Start a business

for £99

Be your own boss – on a budget!

Emma Jones

PEARSON

Harlow, England • London • New York • Boston • San Francisco • Toronto • Sydney
Auckland • Singapore • Hong Kong • Tokyo • Seoul • Taipei • New Delhi
Cape Town • São Paulo • Mexico City • Madrid • Amsterdam • Munich • Paris • Milan

Pearson Education Limited
Edinburgh Gate
Harlow CM20 2JE
United Kingdom
Tel: +44 (0)1279 623623
Web: www.pearson.com/uk

First published 2015 (print and electronic)

© Emma Jones 2015 (print and electronic)

The right of Emma Jones to be identified as author of this work has been asserted by her in accordance with the Copyright, Designs and Patents Act 1988.

Pearson Education is not responsible for the content of third-party internet sites.

ISBN: 978–1–292–06577–9 (print)
       978–1–292–06579–3 (PDF)
       978–1–292–06580–9 (ePub)
       978–1–292–06578–6 (eText)

British Library Cataloguing-in-Publication Data
A catalogue record for the print edition is available from the British Library

10 9 8 7 6 5 4 3 2 1
18 17 16 15

Cover design by Two Associates

Print edition typeset in ITC Giovanni Std 9.5/13pt by 3
Printed by Ashford Colour Press Ltd, Gosport

NOTE THAT ANY PAGE CROSS REFERENCES REFER TO THE PRINT EDITION

Contents

Part 4: Going for growth

About the author

Emma Jones is founder of Enterprise Nation, the UK's most active small business network.

Following a career with an international accounting firm, Emma started her first business at the height of the dot com boom in 2000. That business was Techlocate.com and was successfully sold 15 months after launch.

Emma's next start-up was Enterprise Nation. For the past eight years, the company has helped thousands of people turn their good ideas into great businesses. This happens through a daily blog and online marketplace, lively events, ebooks/books/kits and a campaigning voice to government.

In 2011 Emma was a cofounder of national enterprise campaign, StartUp Britain, which she ran for three years. During that time, the campaign went on national StartUp tours, hosted StartUp events and launched PopUp Britain, filling empty shops with small businesses.

Emma received an MBE for services to enterprise in January 2013 and, in August 2014, was appointed chairman of the Board of Trustees of Plotr, a website that helps young people plot decisions on their future, including self-employment as a key option.

The author of books including *Spare Room Start Up: How to start a business from home*, *Working 5 to 9: How to start a business in your spare time*, *Go Global: How to take your business to the world* and *The Start Up Kit: Everything you need to start a small business*, Emma is one of the UK's leading small business experts.

Visit Enteprise Nation online at **www.enterprisenation.com** or in person at Somerset House in London. There is always something going on for start-ups!

With thanks

Thanks to the companies who agreed to be profiled and quoted in the book.

Profiled companies

Founder	Company
Alison Edgar	Sales Coaching Solutions
Eveline Ip	Doggity
Blake Folgado and Mike Dean	Venteo
Imran Merza	Jealous Sweets
Daniel Roberts	BananaBerry
Angie Spurgeon	Artwork by Angie
George Palmer	SendOwl
Hayley Carr	London Beauty Queen
Kirsty Fate	Luna on the Moon
Sarah Hamilton	Sarah Hamilton Prints
Joanna Zhou	Maqaroon
Simon Jenner	Urban Coffee
Made in the Valley (cooperative)	Made in the Valley
Emma Selby	The Farnham Hub
Christina Richardson	Brand Gathering
Dean Mitchell	Dean Mitchell Photography

Quoted companies

Name	Business
Anna Steyn	Retail Factor
Paula Hutchings	Vision Marketing
Philip Crilly	Eatibbles
Arianna Cadwallader	Saturday Sewing Session
Alex Gooch	Alex Gooch (artisan baker)
Vera Blagev	Vera Vera On The Wall
Emily Coltman	FreeAgent
Clive Lewis	ICAEW
Alison Battisby	Social media professional
Mallory Cravens	Student of entrepreneurship
Lord Young of Graffham	Founder of StartUp Loans

Publisher's acknowledgements

We are grateful to Shutterstock.com for the images which appear in this book:

p.8 © Rusian Grumble; p.20 © RawPixel; p.55 © Evgeny Karandaev; p.67 © MPF photography; p.82 © cmgirl; p.104 © Graphic Store; p.114 © best works; p.170 © Mathias Richter; p.188 © Lightspring

In some instances we have been unable to trace the owners of copyright material and we would appreciate any information that would enable us to do so.

Introduction

There has never been a better time to start a business. I have been saying this since 2000 and will keep repeating until it is no longer the case!

There has never been a better time to start a business

What you will discover in this book is why people in their thousands are starting businesses, every day, from the comfort of home, and how they are embracing technology to start those businesses on a bootstrap of a budget.

This book tells the story of 15 businesses and gives you the steps to come up with an idea, make a plan, make sales, build a brand and be a success. Doing so will require an investment of less than £99, including the cost of this book!

A few months ago, I heard a finance professional speak at an event and say:

> *If you have money, people expect you to pay for stuff.*
>
> *If you have no money, you get a lot of stuff for free.*
>
> (thank you, Jon Bradford of TechStars!)

This statement is brilliant and true.

Across these pages you will learn how to make the most of free technology tools, how to raise your profile with no marketing budget required, how to beg, borrow and barter your way into business and how to access the support on offer from the government, big business and your small business peers.

Over the past decade, I have helped thousands of people start a business; through a monthly StartUp Saturday class and national StartUp events, through a StartUp Kit and a collection of other books, and through campaigning on behalf of start-ups. Across all this activity, my advice has been consistent. That advice is:

Start your business on a budget.

Business owners who start on a budget understand the business basics and importance of keeping costs low and sales high. It stands them in good stead to run a successful enterprise.

If you want to enjoy the freedom, flexibility and financial reward that comes with being your own boss, this book has been written for you. Consider it your guide as you embark upon an exciting and entrepreneurial journey. Starting your business with the help of this book will get your business off to the very best start – starting on a budget!

Emma Jones

Start-up mania hits the UK!

If you have picked up this book thinking now could be the time to take that long-held idea and turn it into a business, or you have had enough of earning for someone else and want to start earning for yourself, then now is an ideal time to take action. And you certainly will not be acting alone.

The UK is experiencing start-up mania! In 2013 a record-breaking 524,000 people turned their idea into a business and this record looks set to be smashed again in 2014. The Office for National Statistics is reporting unseen highs in the number of people opting for self-employment with one in every seven people now working for themselves and 90 per cent of the jobs growth since 2008 being due to self-employment. This is no blip in the economy, either. Enterprise fever is set to continue as surveys show 65 per cent of young people wanting to be their own boss after leaving school/college/university or after some grounding of working first for someone else.

In 2013 a record-breaking 524,000 people turned their idea into a business

Why, you may ask, is this happening? I will give you four reasons:

1. **Personal choice** – students, mums, employees and the recently retired are choosing to become self-employed to benefit from the freedom and flexibility that comes with it. There is no better way to earn a living than doing what you

love and building a business, from home, around the family. Millions of people are doing it and are happier for it. A recent Enterprise Nation survey showed 99 per cent of respondents are more healthy and fulfilled being self-employed than they were as an employee. I want to meet the 1 per cent who are not and ask why!

2. **Open markets** – you do not want to start a business without knowing there is a market of people to buy and, fortunately for the start-up, markets are becoming very particular about what they want to buy and from whom they buy it. Witness the rise of the niche start-up: the new venture that offers a product or service to a clearly identified audience, for example PA services to the food sector or fashion for the music industry. Niche businesses are the very best kind of business, as you quickly become an expert in your field, reach customers and go global. With over two billion consumers online, often looking for British-made and designed products and services, the world is your trading oyster.

3. **Low costs** – whilst popular programmes like *Dragons' Den* give the impression you need to raise thousands or remortgage the house to start a business, the truth is quite different. The majority of people start a business while holding onto the day job to give themselves time to build confidence and cash flow in the business. They are embracing technology and making the most of every offer and asset being opened up for start-ups, to keep costs low. This book is focused on showing you how to do the same.

4. **Support on tap** – there has never been so much support available for start-ups. This is coming from government, in the form of programmes like StartUp Loans, from big business which is opening up accelerators, supply chains and its customer base for the benefit of start-ups, and there is support from peers, too. We are operating in what is referred to popularly as the sharing economy where start-ups share experiences and learning with each other, and more experienced entrepreneurs share their time to offer a guiding and mentoring hand.

This book will help you realise the benefits of self-employment by showing how to access support, make the most of the web, develop a niche and attract customers. It shows how to achieve all this while keeping costs as low as they will go.

In reading the tips and techniques that follow, please bear three important words in mind:

Beg, borrow and barter

These are the three most critical words when starting a business on a budget!

Before paying for anything, think instead about how you can partner to get what you need for free, or pitch to someone who would benefit from lending to or bartering with you.

Become your own boss for less than the cost of a return London to Manchester rail ticket

Add to this all the free and powerful technology tools at your disposal and you will see, as the pages go by, just how straightforward it is to become your own boss for less than the cost of a return London to Manchester rail ticket!

Part

1

Preparation and planning

Every great business starts with time spent on preparing the ground and planning for success.

This involves researching and understanding your market and writing a plan that will guide the business from start-up through to growth.

Chapter

1

Coming up with an idea

To get started, the first thing you need is an idea. They are free to come by; the secret is in the execution!

Ideas can come as a lightbulb or eureka moment but, for most people, it is a case of realising that what you really want from life is to pursue an interest, and make a living from doing what you most enjoy. In terms of coming up with the idea, my advice is to ask yourself these three questions:

1. **Have you spotted a gap in the market?** Have you tried to buy something that you just cannot find? If so, others might be looking for that product or service, too.

2. **What is your passion, hobby or skill?** There is no finer way to start a business than basing it on something that takes your interest, as the working hours will not seem quite so long!

3. **Have you seen someone do something that you think can be improved on?** If so, it could be time to give it a go.

The answers to these questions will help you shape an idea, which can then be tested.

I run a monthly event called StartUp Saturday where, in the space of five hours (on a Saturday), we cover all you need to know to start a business. At the beginning of the day, I ask StartUp Saturday-ers to share their business idea with the group. It is at this point that many ask if they should be sharing their idea at such an early and delicate stage, for fear of someone else stealing it!

My view on this is clear: unless you have come up with a unique invention that needs protection and patents (see the section on

Source: Shutterstock.com, © Rusian Grumble

'intellectual property' in Chapter 4), then you are pretty safe in telling a trusted circle about your idea. Someone else would find it hard to develop the idea in the way you envisage. One of the great assets start-ups have is the power of the story that comes with the idea and you, as the business owner, are a big part of that story – this is something no-one can take away from you.

A start-up I know and love is Claudi&Fin. Started by friends Lucy Woodhouse and Meriel Kehoe, these two ladies launched a business selling Greek-style yoghurt lollies for kids. Their first customer was Sainsbury's, where they are now stocked in over 400 stores. I asked Lucy if Sainsbury's was comfortable dealing with two mums running a business from home when their usual suppliers are huge multinationals. 'The fact we are two mums running a business around the kids is what makes us special and stand out,' was the reply.

The point is, any large company could decide to go into production of frozen Greek-style yoghurt lollies but, what they cannot replicate, is the authenticity and story of the people behind it.

With safety in sharing assured, it's time to test your idea on what I call the Friends and Family Focus Group.

Friends and Family Focus Group

Turn to those you trust to seek their views. Some say you do not get honest feedback from friends and family and, certainly, you will need to speak to potential customers, too. This is covered in the next chapter devoted to market research but, first, ask those you know the following questions:

- Do you like the product/service?
- Would you buy it?
- What would you pay for it?
- Does it suit my skills to run this business?

The result of this focus group could be changes to your product or service as well as having an opportunity to perfect your pitch.

You want to get to a point of describing the idea as articulately as possible for those 'elevator pitch' moments when you have less than a minute to make your mark with potential customers/suppliers/funders/buyers. To achieve this, try a simple exercise of describing your idea in the form of a tweet. This means you have less than 140 characters to get the message across! For example, for Enterprise Nation, it would be:

We help people start and grow their own business, through a daily blog, live events, books and kits, and a campaigning voice to government.

What would yours be?

Your idea in a tweet

Niche is best

When coming up with your idea, try to make it as niche as possible. What I mean by this is, be very clear on **what** you offer and to **whom**.

Be very clear on what you offer and to whom

The benefits of starting a niche business are two-fold:

- **Low marketing costs** – as you know where your customers are, their likes and dislikes, what they are reading/watching/listening and their key influencers.

- **High customer loyalty** – as customers can get what they are after only from you.

Alison Edgar is a good example of the benefits of a niche business.

Case Study

Name: Alison Edgar

Business: Sales Coaching Solutions

For Alison:

When she started her sales coaching business, the plan was to offer all types of sales services to all types of client. Alison soon realised this presented a marketing challenge as she had to run promotions everywhere to reach such a wide market. Her other love in life is small business (as she is one!) so she decided to niche the business and become a sales coach, focused on the small business sector. This immediately refined the marketing plan as Alison only needed to appeal to small businesses so she delivered guest posts on small business blogs, approached small business editors in the press and got involved with government programmes that support small business! What's more, she could introduce her clients to each other.

- ✔ **Marketing costs were minimal** – as she knew exactly where to find her clients and the kind of messages to which they responded.

✔ **Customer loyalty was high** – as not only did Alison deliver the sales coaching promised, she also delivered industry expertise and introductions, i.e. extra value to every client.

When I first set up I didn't think I needed a niche as I considered the skills I had were so transferable that I could support anyone in any business sector. Then I came on to marketing my business and I didn't know where to start. After deciding on my niche market everything fell into place. I have a focus to my business and a focus which I happen to love.

Eveline Ip is another business owner benefiting from the power of niche, as she develops her app directing dog owners to dog-friendly venues.

Case Study

Name: Eveline Ip

Business: Doggity

The idea for Doggity came about in the summer of 2012. I was working as a business analyst for a major outdoor advertising company in London. My husband and I became dog owners and struggled to find dog-friendly venues. There were a handful of websites and forums that included bits and pieces of information, highlighting pubs to hotels and beaches. We saw a gap in the market to pull this information together with a focus on dining venues in urban areas of Britain.

Eveline found a developer and offered him a 10 per cent share in the business in exchange for a discounted cost for developing Doggity's website and app, and it took

▶

three months from the initial idea to having a rough and ready version available on iTunes.

Our market is dog owners in urban areas so we can be selective and reach out to journalists in lifestyle sections of broadsheets and magazines to market the product. Our biggest PR success to date was being included as a top 10 pet-friendly gadget by The Independent. A surge in downloads followed!

Eveline keeps the app updated by keeping an eye on new eateries and venues and contacts them to ask after their dog-friendly policy, with an annual audit to ensure the data is up to date and accurate.

Over the next 12 months the plan is to focus on growing the number of venues, increase the number of downloads and monetise the app.

I heard at an Enterprise Nation seminar the advice that niche is good and that stayed with me. As technology continues to advance, many generalist apps have become redundant. Smaller niches, on the other hand, continue to grow. I'm a big believer that niche is good!

www.doggity.co.uk

@doggityUK

See Chapter 7 for ways to market your idea to a chosen audience, without breaking the bank.

The name game

With an idea in place, it is time to come up with a name and this could just be one of the most time-consuming tasks of your start-up!

When thinking of a name, consider the following:

- Have you got a name that could lend itself to a business? US entrepreneur Martha Stewart has done a fine job of building a multi-billion-dollar business, using her own name.

- Choose something that is easy to spell and translates well across borders if you are looking to go global.

- Check if the name is available by doing an online search, checking domain name and social media availability and using Companies House WebCHeck service at **http://wck2. companieshouse.gov.uk/**.

The name does not have to describe what you do; does McDonald's describe burgers or Apple shout computers? But do think of a name that will sit well with the market you are going to serve.

Think of a name that will sit well with the market you are going to serve

Top tip

Most domain registration websites offer alternative name suggestions when searching for domain availability, which can offer inspiration.

- **GoDaddy: www.godaddy.com**
- **123-reg: www.123-reg.co.uk**
- **1&1: www.1and1.co.uk**

See Chapter 4 for advice on how to protect your name, company brand and the business idea through intellectual property protection.

Investing in an idea

If you really want to start a business but just cannot think of an idea, consider buying into someone else's! This is where direct selling comes up as an opportunity. For less than £100, you can become a consultant, agent or network marketer with some household brands. The benefit of buying into a direct selling opportunity is you are your own boss, with the support of a team of fellow agents on hand. Here are five of the better-known opportunities and the costs of starting in business with their brand.

Brand and product	Cost
Avon Independent Avon representatives sell beauty products via print catalogues and online in their local area. **www.avon.uk.com**	Nothing to pay up front. The start-up fee of £16 is charged to your account after you have placed a first order – this is split into £10 in your first order and £6 in the second order, i.e. you pay the fee after making sales.
Betterware Home supplies are on offer from this company that has been trading for 85 years. **www.betterware.co.uk**	No start-up fee and you receive promotional materials and catalogues to start trading, for free.
The Body Shop At Home Sell gifts, make-up and skincare at home parties or online with a brand that is well-known on the high street. **www.thebodyshop.co.uk/athome**	Consultants are asked to buy a Pamper Kit, which costs £45 and contains £175 worth of products and catalogues so sales can start.

Jamie at Home A party-plan business selling the Jme collection of kitchenware. **www.jamieathome.com**	There are two starter options: • Pay £120 for a starter kit containing £400 worth of products to sell. Payments are split so you pay £50 up front and the remainder after making sales. • Pay £75 for a seasonal starter kit with products worth over £320 and pay £40 up front.
Scentsy Home parties selling perfumes and scented products. **www.scentsy.com**	The starter kit costs $99 and comes with products, catalogues and a personal website so you can launch straight into hosting your first party.

With any of these opportunities, carry out plenty of research before handing over money. Speak to existing consultants and agents to ask if they are earning, and visit online forums to review comments as well as checking if the company is a member of the industry body, Direct Selling Association (**www.dsa.org. uk**).

Total cost of coming up with an idea:

Idea generation	£0.00
Friends and Family Focus Group	£0.00
Coming up with a name	£0.00

Total costs incurred to date: £0.00

Chapter

2

Carrying out market research

With an idea in hand, you want to be clear about the market of customers that is going to buy your product or service. The research should look to discover:

- how many customers are in your market
- their key influencers
- their current suppliers.

Consider the four Cs as your market research guide, shown in the following table.

Customers	Competitors
Are your customers of a certain age, demographic or based in a certain area? What is the size of this customer group in the UK and overseas (if international trade is on your mind)?	Who is currently servicing your market? What are they doing well, and not so well?
Costs	Channels
What price is the customer prepared to pay? Can you charge this, taking into account your own costs?	What are your customers reading/watching/listening to? The answers to this will be your channels to market.

At the StartUp Saturday class, we start the day with everyone introducing themselves and their idea. This was one of the best I ever heard:

Source: Shutterstock.com, © RawPixel

> *I'm a lawyer by day but my real love in life is scuba diving. I've spotted a gap in the market for an app to measure dives. My market is men aged 22 to 35 with high disposable incomes. They read the* FT Weekend *and spend a lot of money on technology and gadgets.*

In one sentence, he was clear on what he was going to deliver, to whom, and the publications they were reading! Know your customers inside out and this will go a long way to reducing your marketing costs.

Know your customers inside out

Here is how to go about the research.

Online research

Search engines

Start with the major search engines to find market reports, popular blogs and forums and the key people talking about your particular topic.

The major search engines are:

- Google: www.google.com
- Bing: www.bing.com

Continuing on from our legal friend above, who is developing an app for scuba divers, typing 'Size of the scuba diving market' into both search engines delivers links to industry reports and popular diving forums.

This gives me a good start to my market search.

Trade bodies

For more refined industry reports, check out trade bodies for the sector in which you hope to operate, as they are highly likely to have industry stats and trends published on their sites. For example, if you are starting a business in fashion, three useful sites and sources of data would be:

- UK Fashion & Textile Association (UKFT): www.ukft.org
- British Fashion Council: www.britishfashioncouncil.co.uk
- British Retail Consortium: www.brc.org.uk

These bodies offer data on customer buying habits, current trends and upcoming opportunities, so represent a valuable (yet free!) resource of data for you.

Regardless of sector, for a more general online search, check out these links.

Link	Research
Alibaba.com **www.alibaba.com** (click on Trade Intelligence)	Business reports and trade knowledge.
Business & IP Centre at the British Library **www.bl.uk/bipc/dbandpubs/Industry%20guides/industry.html**	Industry guides.

▶

DueDil **www.duedil.com**	For researching potential customers and competitors.
IMRG **www.imrg.org**	The UK's online retail association.
Keynote **www.keynote.co.uk**	Market intelligence.
Marketest **www.marketest.co.uk**	Specialist business market research company, but reports do come with a price attached.
Mintel **www.mintel.com**	Consumer data, research, analysis.
Office for National Statistics **www.ons.gov.uk**	Treasure trove of stats relating to consumer behaviour, work patterns, etc. in the UK.
Trendwatching.com **www.trendwatching.com**	Trendspotters across the globe capture new innovations and new markets.
YouGov **www.yougov.co.uk**	Focus on public opinion and voting intentions.

The majority of these research tools are available in the Business & IP Centres at regional city libraries and are free to access. See Chapter 8 for more details on the support you can access from the local library.

Survey tools

Finesse the research by asking potential customers for their views. This can be done with survey tools SurveyMonkey and Wufoo.

- **SurveyMonkey (www.surveymonkey.com)** – here you can compile and send a survey to get the answers you are after. The basic package is free and offers 10 questions and 100 responses per survey, which is sufficient for a first piece of market research. With this basic package, you can collect data via a weblink, email or Facebook, or embed the survey on your website or blog.

- **Wufoo (www.wufoo.com)** – this is a web application, enabling anyone to create online forms. The free account offers access for 1 user to create 3 forms with 10 fields and receive 100 entries.

Here is an example survey you could use:

Question	Answer options
What is your gender?	Male/Female
What is your age?	Open box or include age grade options
Where do you live?	This could be regional choices (e.g. London, North West, Yorkshire) or country (UK, USA, France, Germany) or type of location (town, country)
From where do you currently buy your xxx?	Free text response box
What price do you pay?	Insert options
Are you happy with your current supplier?	Yes/No
If there were improvements you could choose, what would they be?	Options such as: • Free delivery • Ability to buy online • Better customer service • Better price • Larger range • Other
What would encourage you to recommend a new supplier to friends?	Options such as: • Quality product and good service • Introduction fee • Easy to share on social media

What most encourages you to buy?	Options such as: • Recommendation from a friend • Feature in a magazine/on a blog • Professional website and easy check-out • Other

Top tip

Surveys that offer the chance of a prize to people for completing it always attract a better response! Ask around for someone to donate a prize (an iPad, a free stay at a local hotel, a hamper of artisan goods, etc.) in exchange for you promoting them on the survey, and in the results if you are going to publish them. To choose a winner for the prize, ask people to include their email address for a chance to win, and use RANDOM.ORG (**www.random.org**) to pick the prize-winner. The other benefit of this is you get to capture email addresses of potential customers, too!

To promote the survey, email friends, family and potential contacts and customers and promote it to any followers you have on social media. Young app company, Venteo, turned to social media to generate thousands of votes for a funding competition it entered. The same principles apply when asking people to complete a survey/offer views/provide feedback.

Review the responses, as this will help you perfect your idea and offer.

Case Study

Names: Blake Folgado and Mike Dean

Business: Venteo

Blake and his business partner, Mike, came up with their start-up idea when they were out at events with friends, taking pictures, and wondering why there was not a single space in which to share them.

There would always be a group of five or more of us when we would go out and the next day we would always repeat the same thing, asking each other to send one another the pictures from the night before, or looking on each other's phones. That's how I came up with the idea for Venteo, which allows you to have each other's pictures on your phone straight away and all in the same album.

Venteo can be used for any event ranging from a BBQ to a Rolling Stones concert or even a global 'what shoes are you wearing day'. It is just a really easy way for everyone to share their moments and perspective in the same album.

To contribute towards the cost of app development, Blake entered Enterprise Nation's funding competition, Fund 101, to win £500. The competition is based on submitting a winning pitch and then asking friends, fans and followers to vote in support.

We saw Fund 101 not only as great way to win £500 but also as a challenge for us to see how much support we could gain via online methods. The support we received was incredible.

As the app we have created is purely online and requires users, we thought this would be a good test of how we can get people to join in. We focused the majority of our time on Facebook and targeting people

▶

in the Portsmouth and Hampshire area, which is where we are based. The amount of shares we got was just insane and the number of votes just kept on growing!

The exercise was a good test for the young entrepreneurs as they now turn attention to promoting the app.

We've decided to focus on large-scale events. We have already been used for one festival of 80,000 people and have another in a few weeks in the Dominican Republic. We are looking at working with some big artists to allow them to engage with their fans in a new way and also looking at partnering with experimental marketing agencies to allow them to capture the images taken at their stunts. We have been lucky to get featured on some great websites that have helped massively in order to promote the business and app.

We have a big vision and now need to start building the updates to get us closer to it. One thing we will be looking to do soon is raise outside funding to help us grow the business much faster. There's a lot to be done, so no more partying for us!

www.venteo.co

@venteoapp

Offline research

Head out to meet people face to face and ask some questions.

The library

The Business & IP Centre at the British Library in London, and now in six regional cities, is a must-visit at this stage of your start-up. The business-focused centres in the libraries have millions of pounds' worth of research and market intelligence that you can access for free. They also host workshops offering DIY tips and techniques on the art of market research.

It was thanks to Manchester Library that I started my first business, back in 2000, as free hourly internet sessions were on offer. I would book in each day and avidly research for the new venture, without having to break into start-up funds.

Imran Merza is the entrepreneur behind Jealous Sweets and, for him, it was the London Business & IP Centre (**www.bl.uk/bipc/ resmark/index.html**) that gave him the start he needed.

Case Study

Name: Imran Merza

Company name: Jealous Sweets

It was in trying to impress a girlfriend that Imran spotted a gap in the market and came up with the idea for his new start-up.

> *I started dating a girl who loved sweets and was vegetarian and, at the start of our relationship, I was trying to get into her good books by finding her vegetarian sweets. The best sweets contained gelatin, which is derived traditionally from pig, beef and horse hoofs and parts of the animal that we don't usually eat.*

> *As I scoured the internet and shops, I realised no one was making gelatin-free sweets and, when I did come across the occasional brand of vegetarian sweets in health shops, they tasted awful! I also realised that sweets are aimed, branded and marketed towards children. This was when I decided to start a grown-up candy company, taking out the gunk and junk found in traditional sweets. I quit my job and one of my best friends, Taz Basunia, joined me to start the revolution of bringing credibility back to candy.*

Imran and partner Taz had no knowledge of the confectionery market and no idea where to begin but, while searching the web for sweets, Imran had found a link

▶

showing that the British Library had reports on the confectionery industry.

I went along to the BIPC (Business & IP Centre) and started to look at the various reports. The more I researched, the more engrossed I got in the confectionery world. I realised there was very little or no innovation in sweets and they were mass produced, cheap and inferior to chocolate. This research alone gave me confidence that my idea would have some merit and allowed me to build some credibility.

I wanted to know everything I could about the confectionery market; the size, competitors, trends, spending habits, the opportunities and threats of someone starting out with no prior experience. As an outsider, I felt I needed to know everything possible to see if I could really make a splash in the market.

Imran feels this vital research phase gave him the confidence to talk about what he was planning to do and it helped build a blueprint and business plan.

One brick at a time I built the foundation of knowledge. Without this it would be very difficult to sound credible when talking to retailers. It helped me target our audience market and their spending habits and I knew exactly where I would sell our products.

This clear vision has been realised and the company is now selling in Selfridges, Harrods and Harvey Nichols, as well as overseas.

We are starting to export into Europe, Asia and the Middle East and we're getting a lot of interest from other countries, too.

From dating a girl to going global, this is one entrepreneur who spotted a gap in the market after carrying out some serious market research that came absolutely free.

www.thejealouslife.com

@thejealouslife

Hit the streets

One of my favourite start-up stories is the young entrepreneur who wanted to research her market of ladies in their thirties and forties who liked to shop. She knew where to find them and headed to Westfield Stratford City on a busy Saturday wearing a t-shirt that read on the front: 'I'm a start-up', and on the back: 'Don't run away!' With clipboard in hand, she quizzed potential customers on their buying habits and preferences. It gave her the research she needed to perfect her own product and route to market.

Dean Tempest is founder of the best-selling board game, Linkee, that has appeared on *Dragons' Den* and now is selling on the shelves of Tesco, John Lewis and WHSmith, among others. His policy in the research phase was to talk and listen in equal measure.

Talk and listen in equal measure

Whilst juggling our existing jobs we spent a good six months exploring the opportunity, visiting trade shows and trying to find out as much as we could about the industry from research papers and people within the industry. We also held Linkee quiz nights to properly test the product. I would speak about the product to anybody who would listen. It is amazing how many people would say, 'Oh, I know a bloke who's done this, or worked here, give them a call.' I would call them no matter how tenuous the link.

Don't be afraid to get out, meet people and ask for their views. It also worked famously for Innocent, who attended a trade fair with its smoothies, took a stand and wrote above it: 'If you think these smoothies are good enough for us to give up our jobs, place your bottle in the Yes bin.' There was a Yes and No bin at the stand and, by the end of the day, the Yes bin was overflowing. The three founders left their jobs, started Innocent and, in 2013, sold to Coca-Cola at a valuation of over half a billion dollars. It all started by asking people what they thought about the product!

> **Top tip**
>
> Get potential customers involved in your start-up story at an early stage. Create a blog and share the experience you are going through as people will engage with you and want to support and will you on. This is what Philip Crilly did in writing a 12-week start-up challenge for Enterprise Nation, and it was in writing this series that he secured a most high-profile product launch. Read about it in the 'Offline promotion' section of Chapter 7.

Template 1: Market research

The result that you are looking for at the end of this market research phase is a clear understanding of your market. Complete the following template and the job is done.

Customers	Competitors
Number:	Who they are:
Characteristics:	What do they do well:
Potential for growth:	What do they not do so well:
Costs	**Channels**
What people are paying:	Publications:
What people would be prepared to pay with added variety/options/ customer service/twist:	Blogs/forums: Other media: Promotion partners:

Total cost of carrying out market research:

Online search	£0.00
Industry trade reports	£0.00
Research at BIPC libraries	£0.00
Online research via SurveyMonkey and Wufoo	£0.00
Hitting the streets with a clipboard	£0.00
Total:	£0.00

Total costs incurred to date:

Coming up with an idea	£0.00
Carrying out market research	£0.00
Total:	£0.00

Chapter

3

Writing a business plan

A business plan will act as your map. It will guide the business from start to growth, with reference to milestones along the way.

A business plan will act as your map

The plan will include information about how you intend to get started and what your ultimate objectives are – and how you aim to get from one to the other. You might want to start a business and sell it in a few years' time, or grow to a point where you would not want to grow anymore.

Of course, you will need to refer to resources: what you have already, what you will need and how you will pay for it.

So, after coming up with an idea and doing your research, writing the business plan is your first practical step to starting your business. With it under your belt you can say, 'I'm off!'

Or **IMOFF**.

It is an easy way to remember the headings to include in your business plan: Idea, Market, Operations, Financials and Friends. Have these as headings in your plan and you have taken a big step closer to becoming your own boss.

- **Idea:** What is your idea?
- **Market:** Who will be your customers or clients? And who is your competition?
- **Operations:** How will you develop the idea, promote it and provide good customer service?

- **Financials:** Can you earn more than you spend, so that the business makes a profit? Do you need any funds to get started?
- **Friends:** Do you have a support network on hand for when you need business advice? Are there complementary businesses you have identified with whom partnerships are a possibility?

Return regularly to the plan to check progress against targets or to change the plan in response to new opportunities. Here is an example plan and a template for you to complete on your own.

Return regularly to the plan to check progress

Example business plan

Company ABC business plan

Year/date (you may choose to do a 12-month plan, 2 years or up to 5 years)

Contents

Executive summary

The idea

Sales and marketing

Operations

Financials

Friends and family (this title would be more like 'Advisory Board' if preparing the plan for a bank or funder)

Executive summary

Summarise what is in the rest of the plan. Something like this:

The vision for Company ABC is to become the leading company for selling abc to xyz. This plan sets out how the vision will be achieved in the period 2015–2016. It outlines the product on offer, provides data on the market and shows how the company will be operating profitably within the first month.

Having identified a clear gap in the market, I am excited about the opportunity to start and to build a successful business that will offer a quality product [or service] to a well-defined market.

A. Person
Founder, Company ABC

The idea

Include here your 'elevator pitch'; what is your product and how will it benefit the customer?

This is the opportunity to explain the idea of the business in a few sentences.

The market

- **Customers:** Who will be your customers? Include the quantity, their demographic profile, geographic locations, social backgrounds; essentially any strong data that shows you know your audience.

- **Competition:** Who is selling a similar product/service? How do you differ from them? What is your unique selling point? You can do this by producing a table that lists the competition. Outline what makes you stand out in the market: is it that your service will be online, that you will charge a different price, have an innovative marketing approach or offer the service with a special extra twist?

Operations

- **The CEO:** You have come up with the idea for the business and you have done your research on the market. Now it is time for the reader to know a bit about you! Note your background, skills, experience and any credentials for running this business. Plus information on other key members of staff (if there are any).

- **Sourcing:** If this applies to your business, refer to how you will source your product/service. You may be making it yourself!

Sales and marketing

How will you promote what you offer to your customers? Include a brief sales and marketing plan with headings like this:

- **Press** – how many press releases do you plan to distribute each year and to which press channels: newspapers, magazines, radio, etc?
- **Online** – will you have your own blog/website? Mention other sites that you will approach for reciprocal links.
- **Partners** – what about marketing tie-ups with other companies selling to the same audience?

You know where your customers are, so let your marketing plan show that you will reach them in print, online and in person.

Operations

You have sourced the service/product and told customers about it. Refer here to the process customers will go through to buy from you and the systems you will have in place to deliver in time and on budget. Systems may include online ordering and payment, a professional call-handling service to take orders or maybe some specific software.

Financials

Last but not least come the figures. Make this as clear as possible; it is probably best to do it in table form. Drawing up a simple financial forecast will offer the confidence that incoming sales will be higher than outgoings.

Friends and family

In starting and growing your business, will you call on friends and family for advice? If so, refer to this here; mention your board of advisers, your experts-on-call, your support network!

(See Chapter 9 for details on how to access expert advisers and find a mentor whose details you can also include here.)

Use the following template to write your own business plan.

Template 2: Business plan

Idea	What is your product and how will it benefit the consumer?
Market	Customers
	Competition
Operations	CEO
	Systems
	Sales and marketing
Financials	Cashflow forecast
Friends	Team
	Mentors or supporters

Total cost of writing a business plan:

Producing a business plan   £0.00

Total costs incurred to date:

Coming up with an idea   £0.00
Carrying out market research   £0.00
Writing a business plan   £0.00
Total: £0.00

Part

2

Set-up

With the fundamentals of an idea, market research and business plan in place, it is time to get set-up sorted.

Register the company, inform relevant people and bodies, and source the technical kit you need to get this business off the ground and up and running.

Chapter

Taking care of company admin

When starting a business, there are a couple of points of company admin to be considered and acted upon. They revolve around:

- what type of company to form
- who to tell about your new company.

Type of company

There are three main types of company structure in the UK. They are:

1. **Sole trader or self-employed** – as a sole trader, you and the company are a single unit, which means your personal finances are linked intrinsically with the business. Setting up as a sole trader requires telling HM Revenue and Customs and completing a self-assessment tax return every year with a note of your earnings. This status comes with a minimum amount of admin. As a sole trader, you get to keep all the profits from the business but you are also liable for any debt.

2. **Limited company**– starting out as a limited company means you are an employee of the business, which has its own separate legal status. Should anything happen to the finances of the business, you aren't liable personally. To form a limited company, you need to tell Companies House and HMRC, file annual returns and pay Corporation Tax. Limited companies exist in their own right, with the company's finances kept separate from the personal finances of its owners, so your liability is limited.

3. **Partnerships** –this is where two or more self-employed people come together to form a partnership. HMRC views a partnership as: 'Each partner is personally responsible for all the business debts, even if the debt was caused by another partner. As partners, each pays income tax on their share of the business profits through self-assessment, as well as National Insurance.'

Top tip

If you are starting in partnership with a friend, family member or business contact, be sure to have an agreement in place from the start! Download one from online legal sites, such as Clickdocs (**www.clickdocs. co.uk/partnership-agreements.htm**) and include key clauses, such as who owns what, who is responsible for doing what, and what happens in the event of a fall-out. The upside of a partnership is you split the cost of starting the business!

Increasingly, people ask me about community interest companies and social enterprises as a form of company status.

- **A community interest company** is a limited company with a structure designed specifically for social enterprises.
- **A social enterprise** is not a legal term or form of company but instead describes a way of trading as opposed to the structure of the business itself. Social Enterprise UK is the national body for this type of company and describes the status as follows: 'Social enterprises are businesses that trade to tackle social problems, improve communities, people's life chances, or the environment. They make their money from selling goods and services in the open market, but they reinvest their profits back into the business or the local community.'

The body states that, to be a social enterprise a company should:

- have a clear social and/or environmental mission set out in their governing documents

- generate the majority of their income through trade
- reinvest the majority of their profits
- be autonomous of state
- be majority controlled in the interests of the social mission
- be accountable and transparent.

There is a free guide on 'How to start a Social Enterprise' at **www. socialenterprise.org.uk/advice-services/publications/start- your-social-enterprise,** which offers this detail, plus a listing of funding sources, events and awards related to the sector.

Useful links include:

- **Social Enterprise UK: www.socialenterprise.org.uk**
- **Setting up a social enterprise: www.gov.uk/ set-up-a-social-enterprise**
- **UnLtd: https://unltd.org.uk.**

A social enterprise was the status Daniel Roberts chose as a way of doing business in his smoothie start-up.

Case Study

Name: Daniel Roberts

Company: BananaBerry

It was while he was a student that Daniel Roberts came up with his idea for a business.

The idea grew from my involvement as Treasurer of Bristol Social Enterprise (BSE) at University. We had close ties with a number of companies, one of which utilised food waste or 'food that would oth- erwise **become** *waste', as I prefer to put it, to put on cheap meals for students. I liked the concept and so researched the type of food that makes up the over- whelming majority of food waste, which is fruit and veg, and realised that the smoothie – an already*

▶

popular product – was the perfect base on which to build a business. This was the start of BananaBerry.

Daniel launched the company in January 2014, almost three years after first coming up with the idea. After graduating, there were jobs working on logistics at the Olympics, bookkeeping for a hotel in a ski resort and then modelling!

It was the modelling that enabled me to start my company. It gave me a moderate amount of income and a lot of time, both of which I needed.

When it came to the decision to start as a social enterprise, Daniel explains:

I said to myself 'if I can start a company that contributes to improving a social problem (food waste) and donates to a cause that is close to my heart (Cancer Research UK) this early on in my career, then this would make me happy in my work.' I'm also influenced by the fact that being a social enterprise is a strong selling point for a growing number of customers. We can compete against larger companies who do not place as high a weighting in this area and we benefit from the PR angle, too. Some people tie 'social enterprise' to 'not for profit', which is not always the case. We look to create value and profit so we can grow and compete on a larger scale, and so help our cause even more.

Daniel has plans for his social enterprise well laid out.

I want to build a competitive business – not to become the next big smoothie company – but to become the next big social food organisation, offering a variety of products to markets in London. The next 12 months is all about generating a network of customers and contacts so we can run a successful crowdfunding campaign and go for full launch in the summer of 2015. I'm calling it 'The Summer of the Smoothie Life'.

www.bananaberry.co.uk

www.facebook.com/bananaberrysmoothies

@BBsmoothies

When it comes to the company status that most suits you, it is best to speak with a qualified accountant, as everyone's situation is different. Your situation could be earning from the day job and starting a business in your spare time, starting a company that is selling to large businesses, or a new venture that involves lots of export and import. These factors could influence the most ideal company structure, so it is best to seek advice at the outset.

It is best to speak with a qualified accountant, as everyone's situation is different

You can do this at no cost.

The Institute of Chartered Accountants of England and Wales (ICAEW) runs a programme for small businesses and start-ups to access up to three phone calls with chartered accountants, for free. It is called the Business Advice Service and you can search for an accountant local to your area, or specific to your sector.

The Business Advice Service online database can be accessed at **www.icaew.com/en/about-icaew/find-a-chartered-accountant/business-advice-service**.

Over 4,000 firms are participating in the Business Advice Service, giving an hour of their time, at no cost, to help start-ups at the earliest stage. When you're working on a new product, thinking how to get it to market and calculating the finance required to make it work, you could do without having to worry about company structure and tax. This is where an accountant comes in; to help with deciding on the right status and then, as the business grows, more advice that's suited to the stage you're at.

Clive Lewis, head of Enterprise, ICAEW

As money starts to come into the business, I do recommend you hire the services of an accountant. Rules and regulations change frequently and accountants are the experts who follow the changes and can work on the finances at a fraction of the time it would take you. What you have to consider is this: could you be spending time on doing something more profitable, such as sales, marketing or making, as opposed to completing tax returns and calculating payroll? If the answer is yes, it is time to look for an accountant!

Who to tell about your new company

Whichever type of company is selected, the tax man will want to know about your new start-up.

HMRC (HM Revenue & Customs)

- **As a sole trader** – HMRC requests you register with them by 5 October following the end of the tax year for which you need to send a tax return so, for example, register by 5 October 2016 to send a 2015 to 2016 tax return. Register with HMRC and you will receive a Unique Tax Reference number to calculate tax and National Insurance.

  Register as self-employed at **www.hmrc.gov.uk/sa/register. htm.**

- **As a limited company** – register with Companies House (see below) and, if the company is liable for Corporation Tax, you should tell HMRC that the company is active within three months of trading.

  Register a limited company at **www.hmrc.gov.uk/ct/getting-started/new-company/start-up.htm.**

- **As a partnership** – similar to a sole trader, register to complete a self-assessment tax return but, as a partnership, you also complete a partnership supplementary page to show each partner's share of profit/loss.

Companies House

Limited companies are registered with Companies House. If you have decided to set up as a sole trader, you do not need to contact Companies House. There are three ways to register the business with Companies House: online, via a company formation agent or by filing papers. The process and cost of each are shown in the following table.

Form of incorporation	Cost and time
Companies House web incorporation service	Have details to hand, including your company name, office details (director and secretary) and share capital and shareholder details. The cost to incorporate online is £15.
Company formation agent	Have an approved agent register on your behalf and choose from a list of approved suppliers on Companies House website, **www.companieshouse.gov.uk/toolsToHelp/ formationAgents.shtml**. My personal favourite is CompaniesMadeSimple.com which charges £16.99 plus VAT but you also receive £50 cashback if you open a new start-up account with Barclays.
Paper incorporation	Download Form IN01 from the Companies House website, complete and post it to Cardiff. The standard fee is £40 to have documents processed in 8 to 10 days or you can pay £100 for same-day incorporation, see **www.companieshouse.gov.uk/infoAndGuide/ companyRegistrationPaper.shtml**.

> **Top tip**
>
> In April 2008 it became legal to form and run a limited company with just one person, without the need to involve anyone else. Before this, you also needed a company secretary.

- **Local authority** – when starting a business from home, the local authority will want to be sure you are not going to be a nuisance to neighbours! If the house is going to remain pretty much as a residential property, with you quietly going about your business within it, then you will not need planning permission and so do not need to inform the local authority. The test to determine planning permission asks if there will be excess noise, traffic or visitors to the house, as a result of you running a business in it. If you are expecting disturbance around the property, you might want to think about setting up outside the home. Either way, keep the neighbours on side by letting them know what you are doing.

> **Top tip**
>
> Food businesses should contact the local authority to request a visit from a health and safety officer. There is no cost for the visit and the officer's job is to certify your domestic kitchen as a place fit for making food for public consumption. Find details for your Local Authority via the Food Standards Agency website, **www.food.gov.uk/enforcement/yourarea**.

- **Landlord** – when starting a business from home, you may wish to inform your landlord, so you are not in breach of any clauses in the contract saying you cannot run a business from the property. On 15 August 2014 the Government announced a special package to make it easier for people to start businesses from home, including a model tenancy agreement stipulating that landlords cannot withhold consent for running a business from home.

- **Mortgage** – similarly, your mortgage may state that the house cannot be used for a business purpose. Telling the provider may put your mortgage at risk, which is why very few business owners do inform their mortgage provider. My hope is the mortgage industry will see that self-employment is a safer bet than employment and not jeopardise those who decide to start a business from their residential property.

- **Insurance** – with stock and computer equipment at home, and possibly customers visiting, it is better to be safe than sorry and upgrade your domestic home insurance to a home business package.

- **Health and safety** – there is no requirement to contact a health and safety officer (unless you are in the food business, as above) but do carry out a voluntary health and safety risk assessment, which is free and easy to do. Identify any risks in the workplace, such as electric cables from computer equipment, risk of fire, etc. and take steps to limit these risks. You do not need to record or display the risk assessment, unless you employ more than five people. Visit the Health and Safety Executive website for further details, **www.hse.gov.uk/simple-health-safety/workplace.htm.**

A useful link is:

- Government guidance on starting a business from home **www.enterprisenation.com/homebusiness**.

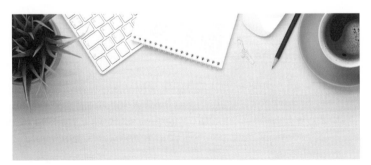

Source: Shutterstock.com, © Evgeny Karandaev

Insuring your home business

Even if you run your business from home, you still need business insurance, as your home insurance is unlikely to cover business activities.

A simple way to buy the cover you need is through a home business insurance package.

With Direct Line for Business this starts from £53 a year and provides peace of mind for potential liabilities you could have to customers' loss of stock or equipment, and also loss of earnings, if something happens that means you cannot run your business from home. There are many different insurance providers offering similar policies.

Top tip

Claim a proportion of home office costs, including council tax, heating, lighting, phone calls and broadband, as allowable expenses against your tax calculation. The amount that can be claimed is from £10 to £26 per month, without the need to show supporting receipts; anything above £4 per week requires supporting documentation. **www.gov.uk/simpler-income-tax-simplified-expenses/ working-from-home**

Telling the boss!

A large number of people are doing what I call 'working 5 to 9', which means keeping hold of the day job and building a business at nights and weekends. This begs the question: should you tell your employer about your new business?

> If you have an employment contract, it most likely says you should not be running a business that has a detrimental impact on the day job. Look out for clauses in your contract that cover 'the employee's duties and obligations', which are likely to refer to you dedicating your 'whole time and effort' to the position of employment.
>
> With this in mind, here is my advice:
>
> *If what you are doing as a business does not conflict with your day job, have a conversation with your employer and stress how the business will not impact the hours and attention you dedicate to work and emphasise that the new skills you are picking up will make you more entrepreneurial in the day job!*
>
> If the employer is amenable, potentially agree to reduce hours at work and increase them in the business.

I will always remember profiling Richard Baldock, the 5 to 9-er who went to tell his boss he was starting a business making a new desk-based product, and her immediate response was to place an order!

If your new business is something that competes with the day job, tread with care. Reputation is everything and you do not want to damage it before you have got going.

When I wrote the book *Working 5 to 9* back in 2010, I spoke to many 5 to 9-ers who had received a promotion in their day job on account of the new abilities and confidence that had come from starting a business, which goes to show becoming your own boss can be good for the career, too!

Reputation is everything

Intellectual property

Something to protect from the outset is your intellectual property (IP). This can be anything from the company logo or font, a product design, or process you have devised. There are four forms of IP and they differ in level of cost and protection:

1. **Patents** – the highest form of IP protection, and the most expensive! This is needed if you have come up with a new invention or way of doing something. For example, Alison Grieve developed a retractable finger receiver incorporated into the underside of a bar tray that stopped it from tipping. She called her invention Safetray and needed patent protection for this unique invention. Protecting a patent can cost thousands of pounds and often requires the services of professional patent attorneys. **www.ipo.gov.uk/types/patent/p-formsfees.htm**

2. **Trademarks** – this is to protect words or logos that distinguish you in the marketplace. Search for existing trademarks on the Intellectual Property Office website (**www.ipo.gov.uk**) and you can apply online, too. The cost to register a trademark starts at £170.

3. **Copyright** – used extensively in the creative sectors, copyright protects assets such as song lyrics, software or photographs. Copyrighting your work means no one else can reproduce it without your permission. The upside is it is free and you do not have to apply. I once heard a presentation from Johnny Earle, founder of highly successful fashion brand, Johnny Cupcakes, reflecting on how he started in business on a budget. Keen to protect his style and brand, Johnny would include the copyright logo on his t-shirts, which cost nothing and, he hoped, dissuaded imitators from copying. It worked and, when he had budget, Johnny upgraded his IP protection to invest in something more sturdy!

4. **Design** – this is how a product looks and the Intellectual Property Office explains the benefits of registering: 'A Registered Design grants exclusive rights in the look and appearance of your product. You can stop people making, offering, putting on the market, importing, exporting, using or stocking for those purposes, a product to which your design is applied.' Registering a design also means you can

make money from selling the design. It costs £60 to apply to register a single design and £40 per design for every additional design.

IP protection	Cost
Patent	Potentially thousands of pounds to protect a unique invention.
Trademark	Protect words or logos with costs starting from £170.
Copyright	Free and no application required.
Design	Connected to the look and appearance of a product. Cost of £60 for the first design and £40 for each extra design.

Useful links include:

- **The Institute of Trade Mark Attorneys: www.itma.org.uk @itmauk**
- **The Chartered Institute of Patent Attorneys: www.cipa.org.uk @TheCIPA**
- **Anti Copying in Design: acid.uk.com @ACID_tweets**

Top tip

Attend free IP events hosted at Business & IP Centres in major city libraries to understand more about the topic and how you can be protected.

www.bl.uk/bipc/workevents/intellprop.html

Angie Spurgeon's business is based on selling designs and this artistic entrepreneur is now successfully selling to national retailers including Waterstones and the National Trust. It was on maker marketplace, Folksy, that she was first discovered.

Case Study

Name: Angie Spurgeon

Business: Artwork by Angie

Back in 2010 I created my first range of illustration prints and greetings cards. Around that time my youngest daughter had just started nursery and, even though I was freelancing on occasional marketing projects, I had a burning desire to use the extra working hours to make a go of launching my own range of illustration-based designs. I was familiar with handmade marketplace Folksy, and felt it was the ideal place to give it a go and see if anyone would be interested. I opened a Folksy shop, website, blog and Facebook page within the space of a couple of months. By using a combination of those four, it really helped get my business off the ground.

After a few months of trading on Folksy, Angie received a message from a publishing company specialising in greetings cards. They had spotted a particular design and wanted to know if Angie was able to create a range of card designs in the same theme and style that they could license and sell to their clients and take to trade fairs.

This was something I was very keen to do, as part of my plan at that time was to try and build collections of designs, which would be ideal to license out and enable me to concentrate on the work I enjoy most – creating illustrations. After some lengthy chats with the publishers, I felt that producing 12 speculative designs

---

for them to take to Autumn Fair International 2011 was a risk worth taking, as I knew those designs would get a chance to be seen by the key buyers in the greetings card sector.

The risk paid off, as both Waterstones and the National Trust placed orders for Angie's range at the fair and this artistic entrepreneur has been working closely with the same publishers, Art Eco Designs, ever since.

Rather than have an agent represent her, Angie decided to self-represent and negotiate her own terms with Art Eco designs. There are two main ways in which a licensing agreement works, explains Angie:

✔ a set-up fee plus royalties of an agreed percentage on each sale or

✔ a flat fee for agreed usage terms.

Whichever way the agreement is set up, it needs to reflect a fair deal for both parties, based on the agreed length of time of the licence, the territories for distribution, the type of products the designs can be used on and the amount of exclusivity the licensee is granted for the designs.

It is working for Angie and she plans to continue building the business in this way.

My long-term aim is to try and get designs licensed and produced at a higher volume, as I know that's where the main income for my work will come. It's a balance between commissioned work and licensed work that keeps my business going. I believe it's easier to sell a design for licence if you can prove that it's already popular and sells well – which is where a marketplace like Folksy comes into its own, as it's very transparent about what products are popular and which ones sell.

When it comes to advice for creative businesses wanting to sell original designs to large retailers, Angie suggests:

▶

> *Produce good, original work and then get it out there to be seen. The most important thing is the quality of the product. Get that bit right and then selling to a large retailer becomes a whole lot easier because the product does all the talking and you'll soon find partners to help do the selling for you, allowing you to concentrate on making more great products.*

www.artworkbyangie.com

Artwork by Angie on Folksy: https://folksy.com/search/items?t=items&q=artwork+by+angie&commit=Search

@artworkbyangie

Total cost of taking care of company admin:

Consult with accountant	£0.00
Register as sole trader	£0.00
Register as limited company	£15.00 (online at Companies House)
Notify landlord/local authority, etc.	£0.00
Insurance	£5.00 (for first month)
Intellectual property	£0.00 (to ascertain copyright)
Total:	£20.00

Total costs incurred to date:

Coming up with an idea	£0.00
Carrying out market research	£0.00
Writing a business plan	£0.00
Taking care of company admin	£20.00
Total:	£20.00

Chapter

5

Technology set-up

Technology and the internet are the key ingredients that enable you to start a business on a budget.

For the purposes of this book, I am working on the basis that you have a phone and access to a computer or laptop. If you do not own a computer, head to the local library where you can use one for free. Complement this with a host of free technology tools to help with branding, promotion and sales. These tools are presented in the following sections and a complete listing of all the technology you need follows later in the chapter.

First, we look at the technology set-up in your office, and the kit required so that you can work on the move. In later sections we cover technology to promote the business (emails, social media), sell products and services (marketplaces, website) and manage operations (project management and finances.) You will be surprised by just how much is available for free.

You will be surprised by just how much is available for free

To get going, you will need connectivity in the form of broadband or Wi-Fi.

Broadband

There are two main types of broadband: ADSL broadband offered by companies such as BT and Sky and cable broadband from companies such as Virgin Media. The main difference is that

ADSL broadband requires a phone line while cable broadband does not, meaning you can make a saving with cable on not having to cover the cost of installation and monthly rental of a landline phone.

When reviewing broadband deals, look out for contract terms (i.e. how long will the price of the package remain at the advertised price), review any caps on usage and consider an offer that comes with customer support, especially if you are a first-time user.

Use a price comparison site such as uSwitch (**www.uswitch. com**) to view the best deals in your area and consider opting for a business grade package (even if starting from home) so you get the quality of service you are after. It is when connectivity goes down in the business that you realise just how much you need it!

Top tip

Work on free Wi-Fi hotspots outside the office. Most major coffee shops offer Wi-Fi for free, as do libraries, shopping centres and some hotels. See Chapter 8 for details on workspace that comes complete with technology on tap and check hotspots through sites including:

- **The Cloud: www.thecloud.net**
- **O2 Wifi: www.o2.co.uk/connectivity/free-wifi**
- **BThotspot finder: www.btwifi.com/find/uk.**

Hardware

Kit out your start-up with the basic materials: a computer and phone.

Computer

At the start of the business, using the family computer or laptop will be just fine but, as sales come in and data requirements rise, consider buying a device that is dedicated to the business. As the performance of devices has increased, prices have decreased and

Source: Shutterstock.com, © MPF photography

now you can get a budget laptop for around £400. When making the purchase, these are the things to look out for:

- **Processor** – this determines the speed of your computer so, the higher the number, the faster it can run.
- **Memory** – memory is referred to as RAM and you want as much of it as possible so you can run more programs at once.
- **Hard drive** – this is the part of the device that gives you space for data and programmes. It can be expanded with an external hard drive, but look for something from the start that gives you the space needed to grow.

Ask for device recommendations from friends and peers or visit trade websites such as PCAdvisor or PC Magazine and search for reviews on the best budget laptops or view options on deals site Huddlebuy.

Useful links include:

- PC Advisor: www.pcadvisor.co.uk
- PC Magazine: www.pcmag.com
- Huddlebuy: www.huddlebuy.co.uk/deals

> ## Top tip
>
> Look out for small business surveys and compe-
> titions that give away gadgets as a prize or incentive.
> Enterprise Nation has given at least 15 devices away to
> lucky survey winners over the years!

Phone

You are likely to have a smartphone already – over 70 per cent
of people in the UK do – but have you also considered a VoIP
phone? This stands for voice over Internet Protocol and it means
making calls over the internet as opposed to a phone line. As
such, it is a cheaper way of making calls, is sometimes free and
the easiest way to set up a second line. You can buy a VoIP phone
handset from electrical stores such as Maplin for £10 or simply
speak directly into the microphone in your laptop that now
comes as standard.

The most well-known VoIP providers are Skype and Vonage.
Signing up to Skype allows you to make free calls to other Skype
users, and to landline or mobile phones for a small fee. You can
host group video calls and assign a landline-sounding phone
number to your Skype account, to receive calls at the computer or
divert to the mobile when out and about. The same benefits come
with Vonage for which you pay a monthly fee of £7 as opposed to
pay-as-you-go credit with Skype.

Useful links include:

- **Skype: www.skype.com/en/business**
- **Vonage: www.vonage.co.uk**

  *With staff, consultants and sponsors based around the world, we
  communicate through regular Skype calls, instant messaging and
  email. For team members we use Google calendars (shared) and
  Google Docs. We also use normal phones – mainly when we're being*

lazy. We haven't invested in any software or communication tools because we haven't needed to. It's all free.

Luke Brynley-Jones, Our Social Times

Top tip

Communicate with partners and suppliers on WhatsApp. This is a cross-platform (i.e., it works on any device) messaging app that means you can communicate instantly with WhatsApp groups you create. You do not have to pay for sending messages and WhatsApp is free to download and costs $0.99 after a year.

www.whatsapp.com

Accessorise!

As budget in the business grows, expand the office kit to include extras such as a printer, webcam, speakers and, maybe, an additional screen display. You are likely to be spending a lot of time in the office, so equip it for your enjoyment!

Ahead of making any early purchase, consider one of the mainstays of this book: 'Beg, borrow and barter.' If someone has the kit you are after, ask if you could borrow it for a couple of months as you find your feet. Could you work out of someone's office, in exchange for building their website/doing their marketing etc.? Avoid having to incur the cost until the money is in the bank – in the meantime, make a case to those who have kit, for you to use it, borrow it or share it temporarily.

Beg, borrow and barter

Alex Gooch is an artisan baker and the kit he needed when starting out was an entire kitchen! He turned to his employer to ask for help.

I was the head chef at a privately owned hotel. When I stopped working for them with the intent to start my own business, they kindly let me use the kitchen in the hotel at night. It was challenging at times, as I would have to bake through the night and then make sure I was out and the place cleaned and ready for them to use in the morning! This space enabled me to test run my breads and it gave me the confidence to seek the investment and look for and set up my premises and business.

Software

Software is the programs and operating system that are used by your computer. Many of the programs are now hosted in the cloud, which means you can access your documents, notes, emails and files from anywhere. Cloud applications have brought down costs for small businesses, as there is no upfront investment required and you do not need expensive servers to host the software, as it lives on the internet. Cloud apps do not take up space on your computer and you do not have to worry about backing up your data. They are also, more often than not, free to use.

Cloud applications have brought down costs for small businesses

Here are 10 of the best.

Ten cloud apps for business

1. **Office 365 (www.microsoft.com/office365).** The industry standard in office software, this comes with Word, Excel, PowerPoint, Outlook and other applications on a monthly subscription basis. With Office 365 you can also share files and host online meetings.

2. **Google Docs (docs.google.com).** This includes apps for word processing, spreadsheets, presentations, drawings and forms – all the apps run inside your browser rather than on your desktop. All of your work is stored in the cloud and it is easy to collaborate with others in real time on the same document.

3. **Gmail and Google Calendar (mail.google.com, calendar. google.com).** Access emails with Gmail and keep on top of diary dates with Google's calendar software. Both are really useful if you plan to work on the move.

4. **Dropbox (www.dropbox.com).** Dropbox is like a thumb drive in the sky. It is a folder that sits on your computer, but its contents are stored remotely and synced across other computers and devices that are signed into your Dropbox account. No-nonsense sharing, if you are working with others, and peace of mind that all your work is backed up.

5. **Google Analytics (www.google.com/analytics).** When your website is up and running, you will want to know how many people are visiting. Google Analytics, like most of Google's services, is free, and helps you understand your website statistics, including where your visitors are from, which pages they visited the most and how they found your website in the first place.

6. **Hootsuite (www.hootsuite.com).** If social media is part of your marketing plan – and it probably is! – there is no better way to manage your social media presence than with Hootsuite. It keeps you on top of your Twitter, Facebook and LinkedIn accounts, as well as what your customers and potential customers are saying about your business.

7. **Evernote (www.evernote.com).** Evernote is a bit like Dropbox, but for your brain. It helps you 'remember everything' by allowing you to capture notes and ideas, photos and screen grabs, sounds and links, sync them automatically to the cloud and access them from practically anywhere – great for the planning stages of your business.

8. **Trello (www.trello.com).** There is so much to do when starting a business, but you can keep on top of all your tasks with Trello. This is like a Pinterest for tasks and ideas and can be shared with others.

9. **Basecamp (www.basecamp.com).** If some tasks involve other people and form part of larger projects, check out project management software Basecamp. It allows you to share

files, deliver projects on time and keep communication organised and out of your inbox.

10. **MailChimp (www.mailchimp.com)**. To make sure your business message is in other people's inboxes, put together a newsletter with MailChimp, send it out to your customer mailing list and track its success. Just make sure people have signed up to your mailing list before hitting 'send'!

App	Cost
Office 365 **www.microsoft.com/office365**	Access a free trial and then choose from packages that start at £3.10 per user, per month, up to £8 per user. **http://office.microsoft. com/en-gb/business/ compare-office-365-for- business-plans-FX102918419. aspx**
Google Apps for Work **www.google.com/apps**	£3.30 per user, per month. **www.google.co.uk/intx/en_ uk/enterprise/apps/business/ pricing.html#faqs**
Gmail and Google Calendar **(mail.google.com; calendar. google.com)**	Gmail is a web-based email system that enables you to pick up mail on the go, and Google's calendar software is also ideal for working on the move as you can see where you have to be, and when. Free to use.
Dropbox **www.dropbox.com**	Dropbox Basic is free or upgrade to the business version for £11 per user, per month.
Google Analytics **www.google.com/analytics**	Free to use.
Hootsuite **www.hootsuite.com**	Free version available or upgrade to the business package for £9.99 per month.

Evernote **www.evernote.com**	Free version available or upgrade to the business package for £8 per month.
Trello **www.trello.com**	Free version available or upgrade to the business package for $5 per user per month.
Basecamp **https://basecamp.com**	Sixty-day free trial and prices then start at $20. See page 179 for additional project management tools and costings.
MailChimp **www.mailchimp.com**	Access the 'Entrepreneur' package for free to send 12,000 emails to 2,000 subscribers. See Chapter 7 for additional email tools and costings.

Small businesses can now benefit from the same technology that FTSE 100 companies use. With Microsoft Office 365 you always get up-to-date versions of applications and they are accessible from anywhere. The beauty of the subscription model is that there are no large upfront costs to buy software – you pay monthly. Security is increased as updates are all done automatically, making sure the software (and client/business information) remains secure.

Gemma Wood, small business customer marketing manager, Microsoft

With broadband connected, a laptop in use and these free cloud apps at your disposal, you are all set up and kitted out to take on the start-up world.

Total cost of technology set-up:

Broadband	£2.50 per month (i.e. £30 per annum)
Wi-Fi	£0.00 (free hotspots)
VoIP phone	£0.00
Office software	£0.00 (based on free trial)
Total:	£2.50

Total costs incurred to date:

Coming up with an idea	£0.00
Carrying out market research	£0.00
Writing a business plan	£0.00
Taking care of company admin	£20.00
Technology set-up	£2.50
Total:	£22.50

Part

3

Start selling and get known

You started out by selling to friends and family. Now let us take this wider and have your product or service sold to customers across the globe. The more you are talked about, the more likely customers are to buy. We look at how to achieve sales and profile; realising both on a budget.

Chapter

6

Making sales

As an American professor of entrepreneurship once said to me,' If you aren't making sales, you are not in business.' It is a simple statement and very true!

Selling is something not everyone likes to do but comfort yourself with the fact that, with the right product or service, sales is a numbers game and with a target list of, say, 50 prospects, you absolutely will make a sale. You just have to pitch it well and be persistent!

If you aren't making sales, you are not in business

Pitch perfect

These are the steps to make your perfect pitch.

1. **Make a list** – draw up a list of the people/companies/organisations you think would be interested in buying your product or service. Make a list in Excel, which looks like this.

Company name	Contact	Email	Date contacted	Status
Company ABC	Joe Bloggs	Joe. bloggs@ abc.com	1 Feb 2015	Proposal submitted
Company DEF	Sarah Brown	SB@def. com	18 Jan 2015	SB requested call-back in March

▶

Etc.				
Etc.				

Maintain this as your business development pipeline and review it every week to ensure you are on track in following up leads and keeping in contact with potential clients.

2. **Make it personal** – when contacting someone to make a sale, clearly outline the benefits. Will buying your product or service make the consumer happier, richer, healthier, more productive, successful, etc.? If so, make this clear! Avoid group emails and, when contacting someone for the first time, address them personally and keep it brief. There will be time for more detail later, as your prospect shows interest. The first goal is to attract their attention.

Top tip

Before clicking 'send' on a sales email or 'publish' on sales materials, read through the text and see how many times you have used the word 'you' versus 'I' or 'we'. As the purpose of sales materials is to be clear on the benefits to the consumer, you will want to see more uses of the word 'you' to be sure you're getting that across!

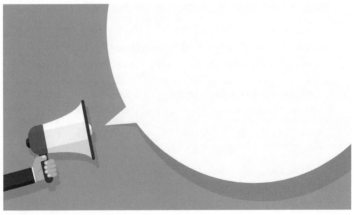

Source: Shutterstock.com, © cmgirl

3. **Offer a clear call to action** – in print and digital promotion, outline the benefits, personalise the approach and offer a clear call to action for the recipient. For example, do you want the potential customer to: follow you on Twitter, enter a competition, dial a number, join a Facebook group, visit your stand, etc? Offer clear instructions on what you would like the prospect to do and make it as easy as possible for them to activate/join/follow.

Persist!

It is a rare day when a customer replies to a first email saying, 'Thank you. I'd love to buy!', so you have to be the one to follow up. Persist in making contact but not so much so that you become a nuisance! Keep in gentle contact, invite prospects to events, add them to a newsletter mailing list and build a relationship so, as soon as the customer is ready to buy, they turn to you.

Build a relationship

> **Top tip**
>
> When making a sales call, do so while standing up and smiling. You will come across as much more confident and optimistic.

With these general principles in mind, here is how you can start selling on a budget.

Online sales

There are three main routes to selling online, on a budget, which are:

1. via a blog
2. via a marketplace, or
3. via a template website.

Blogging

A blog is a great way to get started online. It offers an outlet to share views and expertise and is a route to attracting friends and followers. Over the past few years I have watched with interest as entrepreneurs we have profiled in books and at events have turned their blogs into successful businesses. Entrepreneurs like Kat Williams of RocknRoll Bride (**www.rocknrollbride.com**), Tilly Walnes of Tilly and the Buttons (**www.tillyandthebuttons. com**) and Alex Johnson of Shedworking (**www.shedworking. co.uk**).

What they have all successfully done is follow a process of:

- **Content** – writing and producing content for a specific audience
- **Community** – attracting readers, fans and followers who are interested in this content
- **Commerce** – once a sense of community has developed, and with trust in the brand, they commercialised the relationships.

If you commercialise the blog too soon, you run the risk of losing site visitors who are put off by irrelevant ads or too much sales push, before they have got to know you.

Tilly Walnes explains how she has successfully commercialised her blog and passion for DIY sewing:

My readers love to discover fabric shops, sewing schools and related businesses, so I have a sponsorship programme on the blog that advertises hand-picked businesses that fit the interests of my audience. Following reader requests to share my garment designs, I launched a small line of stylish dressmaking patterns, which are supported by refreshingly clear instructions aimed at beginners. I recently wrote my first book, Love at First Stitch *(May 2014, Quadrille), so the advance on royalties has provided a nice cushion for a while. Plus I teach workshops in partnership with sewing schools and do the occasional paid public speaking gig.*

The most effective form of marketing for me has been to blog strong content regularly – to create posts that I know my readers will love, and to stay on their radar.

To start blogging, choose a free blogging platform:

- **Blogger (www.blogger.com)** – requires a Gmail or Google account.
- **WordPress (www.wordpress.com)** – open source and the most popular publishing platform.
- **Tumblr (www.tumblr.com)** – 198 million blogs now created via this platform!

When it comes to making money from the blog, here are your options.

Sell space

Create a media rate card to sell space on your blog to advertisers interested in reaching the audience you attract. Key details to include in the rate card are:

- number of visitors to the blog/site
- time spent on the site
- social media following
- key characteristics of your community, i.e. age, social status, location, etc.
- upcoming features
- advertising and sponsorship opportunities.

Source the data that you need on site traffic and dwell time from Google Analytics (**www.google.com/analytics/**) and consider a free snapshot TweetReach report (**http://tweetreach.com/about/products/snapshots**) to showcase your social media reach, too.

Have the rate card available on your site and, in a more proactive way, share it with PR companies, media agencies and directly with the brands that have the products and services your audience wants to know about.

Sell sponsorship

There has never been a better time to approach large companies and pitch your start-up as a contender for some of their marketing budget.

Let us take an example of a new start-up creating a blog and community for open water swimmers and let us say Adidas has shown an interest in the rise of the open water swimming movement. The start-up could approach Adidas to suggest sponsorship options as follows.

- **A survey** – using the free survey tools outlined earlier (see Chapter 2), a survey of open water swimmers would deliver intelligence to Adidas on kit requirements and how the sport fits into people's lives. Survey results offer the basis for a good press release, along the lines of: '65 per cent of open swimmers say they have become more ambitious in their career since taking up the sport' and/or infographics to be shared socially.

- **A report** – charting the rise of open water swimming and its potential to be adopted even further in the UK, complete with case studies and imagery, which showcases members of the community.

- **Event series** – delivering talks and coaching for wannabe open water swimmers.

The benefit to you, the start-up, is receiving sponsorship income, an opportunity to find out more about your audience, generate new content, and have the results and your new brand promoted via the national media network of a big brand. The benefit to the big brand is association with a hot new start-up, an objective voice saying open water swimming is on the rise, and access to a number of potential new customers.

In short, everyone wins.

> **Top tip**
>
> To find contacts in large corporates who you think will be interested in your community, visit the media or news section on the corporate site and look for media or PR contacts. Pitching a sponsorship suggestion to the marketing department is a good place to start and most companies have media contacts clearly on display. Failing that, look for corporate executives on LinkedIn. If you don't get an instant response, be persistent and follow up!

Sell product

Turn browsers into buyers by plugging a payment tool into your blog. This could be sales of physical or digital products. Returning to the example of the open water swimming blog, an online shop could sell:

- swimwear
- equipment
- affiliate fees from recommended hotels close to open water lakes
- trips (plugging into online ticketing service Eventbrite)
- coaching with experts
- images and posters of open water locations.

Ensure the products are relevant for your visitors and take your pick of payment tools from the following suggestions:

- **PayPal (www.paypal.co.uk)** – over 140 million people currently shop with PayPal and, with this tool, you can accept payment by debit card, credit card or PayPal account.
- **Stripe (www.stripe.com)** – a cross-device payment form with support for single-click payments. Stripe provides you with APIs that work across desktop and mobile.

- **Worldpay (www.worldpay.co.uk)** – the UK's leading payment provider and with it you can accept all credit and debit cards in person or online.

- **SagePay (www.sagepay.co.uk)** – allows you to accept payments through many different mediums and there is a special step-by-step guide for start-ups.

- **WP eCommerce (https://wordpress.org/plugins/wp-e-commerce)** – a plug-in for WordPress blogs that enables you to sell digital downloads, physical stock or subscriptions.

- **Gumroad (www.gumroad.com)** – for independent writers, designers, game developers, musicians, film makers, artists and anyone in between.

Case Study

Name: George Palmer

Business: SendOwl

Bootstrapped ecommerce platform, SendOwl, was launched as a delivery tool for any business selling digital products. Founder, George Palmer, outlines the business and its benefits.

I was freelancing and had always had an interest in starting my own business. I was searching for the right project when I bought an ebook and couldn't believe how bad the delivery system was. Being a programmer, I realised I could create a better version and started looking into that instead of my original idea.

SendOwl is a delivery system that can work with any website, blog, email system, social media account or anywhere else for that matter. You simply paste a link, which adds a Buy Now or Add to Cart button to your site or blog, and you can start selling digital products right away and across the globe. Once customers choose to buy your product, they are taken through the checkout process, which is mobile-optimised as well as multi-language to increase your conversion rates.

We automatically deliver the file to your customer as soon as they've paid and can cut off the link once the file has been downloaded so it can't be shared.

SendOwl is run as software as a service, so it is a flat monthly fee for each month you are selling. This means that we don't penalise you for growing your business. The level of fee depends on how many products you sell and the size of the files, with the basic package starting from $9 per month.

www.sendowl.com

Sell yourself!

As the blog takes off, you are becoming an expert in your field and a valuable commodity. Make sales through speaking or consulting fees, hosting workshops or turning your blog into a book, which many successful bloggers have done, including Tilly and the Buttons and Shedworking, among others.

Hayler Carr started her blog out of boredom. Little did she know it would turn into a fully fledged business.

Case Study

Name: Hayley Carr

Business: London Beauty Queen

Bored one day in April 2010 and waiting for a new job to start, Hayley Carr decided on a whim to give blogging a go.

I'd worked in the beauty industry for many years and blogs had just started to take off and get noticed by brands. In an arrogant way, I looked at a lot of them and thought I could probably do it better – so London Beauty Queen, LBQ, was born! I never expected it to

▶

evolve into the beast it is today, nor did I ever expect to be making a living from it.

Hayley chose Blogger as her blogging platform.

At the time Blogger was the main platform and the easiest to use. It's what every other blogger I knew used and it was incredibly easy to design with no skills required. Since then it's evolved with me and I haven't needed to change.

To manage the growth of the site, Hayley left her job in 2013 and went full time on the business, which has two main arms – the blog and consulting work with beauty brands.

I removed all advertising from my site in early 2014, as it didn't work for me; it interrupted my readers' journey and took away from the branding I'd created. Similarly affiliate (or commission-based) schemes are quite small as beauty is so easy to pick up on the high street. The majority of my income comes from collaborations, sponsored posts, consulting and working with brands on a more strategic level.

To maintain visitors, interest and income, Hayley blogs several times a week and is acutely tuned in to what her audience is after.

The key to being a great blogger is taking inspiration from everything, everywhere. I read magazines, other blogs, talk to people, spend a lot of time on Twitter and take inspiration from comments and questions from readers. I'm motivated by the fact that this is now my job, so I have to make it work – although I would stop the day I didn't enjoy it any longer. The biggest motivation is the feedback I get from readers; knowing I've helped someone make an informed choice is second to none.

When it comes to plans for this beauty blogger over the next 12 months, Hayley is looking to grow the blog and business into a brand in its own right.

I'm focusing on working more strategically and on long-term partnerships, as well as growing the site and my influence. I've just started working with an assistant and an agent, so hopefully 2015 will bring bigger and better things. I'd love to collaborate with brands on my own makeup accessories line, or become an ambassador for a brand I respect. Other than that I guess I just want to continue to love what I do and make a difference.

www.londonbeautyqueen.com

@LBQblog

Facebook.com/londonbeautyqueen

Pinterest.com/lbqblog

Marketplaces

Upload products and services to powerful marketplaces that attract customers on your behalf and pay only listing fees or commission once you have made a sale. Here are 12 major marketplaces that offer a route to national and international markets.

1. **eBay (www.ebay.co.uk)** – with 145 million active buyers globally, eBay is one of the world's largest online marketplaces. In the UK, the site is home to over 200,000 businesses selling to 18 million shoppers with an item bought every second via the eBay app. Of the 200,000 UK businesses operating on eBay.co.uk, 81 per cent of them sell internationally to four or more countries. Companies sell everything from fashion and furnishings to electricals and collectables on this mega marketplace. To create a listing, just click 'Sell' at the top of most eBay pages (@eBay_UK).

2. **Elance (www.elance.com)** – upload your professional services detail to Elance, which has been around since 1999 and, following a merger with oDesk in 2014, the combined company is now the global leader in online work. More than 2.5 million businesses tap into Elance and oDesk to find,

hire and pay freelancers, with a choice of 8 million people. 'We see more than 2.7 million jobs posted every year and are expecting more than $900 million worth of work to be completed via our sites in 2014. On the freelance side we have skilled professionals providing over 2,500 skills from mobile and web development to design and illustration to writing, translation, SEO, legal and much more.'

To sign up as a freelancer, visit www.elance.com/q/find-work or click 'Want a job? Sign up!' on the oDesk site (@elanceuk, @oDesk).

3. **Enterprise Nation Marketplace (www.enterprisenation. com/marketplace)** – small business network, Enterprise Nation (my own company!) has launched a marketplace to match small businesses with talented professionals and advisers. If you are a supplier of advice on sales and marketing, making the most of digital technologies, access to finance or management and leadership, create a profile for free and be matched with small business owners looking for the advice you offer (@e_nation).

4. **Etsy (www.etsy.com)** – 'an online marketplace where people around the world connect to buy and sell unique goods'. Sellers span more than 150 countries and there is a community of 30 million buyers. Etsy is a thriving marketplace where sellers, artists and creators all come together to share their work and ideas with one another. The site has a blog, which highlights new product launches, plus featured sellers and debates on various topics. Forums feature strongly on the site. To start selling on Etsy, you need to register for an account, which requires a credit card and valid email address for verification purposes. For anyone who makes handmade items, the power of this global platform cannot be denied (@etsyuk).

Case Study

Name: Kirsty Fate

Business: Luna on the Moon

Kirsty Fate is founder of Luna on the Moon; a brand that sells on Etsy and wholesale across the globe. Kirsty has been a maker for as long as she can remember.

From the 'works of art' I used to paint my mother to hang in her doctor's surgery to trying to make a glittery sneaker cake for a friend's birthday, I've always been making and trying my hand at things. I even recently purchased my very own drill!

Kirsty did not start selling any of her creations until she was encouraged to do so by her now husband and business partner, Steve. The business started small and started selling on Etsy.

Etsy was not as well known when we first joined in 2011 but a friend had suggested it and it seemed like a great platform to begin with, to open up our very tiny business to a worldwide market. Our sales have increased and, in the past six months, around 40 per cent of our sales have come from outside the UK. It used to be more but, as Etsy's profile in the UK is growing, so is the volume of UK-based orders.

Kirsty also started out by selling at markets, which provided valuable feedback in the early stages of the business.

We did a range of markets from your more local independent type to social events and to the big established names like Portobello Road. We would definitely recommend everyone with a small business to try and see what works for them but, for us, we now do a lot better concentrating on online and wholesale sales with the sporadic market to gauge people's

▶

> *responses to our products. Nothing can beat face-to-face responses, where you can see people engage with the product.*
>
> *We also sell wholesale and are currently stocked in Dubai and LA. Both these stockists approached us through social media. We have big plans in the future to build on this list.*

To promote the Etsy store, Kirsty turns to social media to drive traffic.

> *Social media is crucial and is our main marketing channel. My personal favourite is Instagram but we also have a presence on Facebook, Twitter, Pinterest and Tumblr. I cannot stress how invaluable social media is for building a fan base and for promoting your brand. Lately we have seen a big rise in sales coming from Instagram, so it proves this works!*

Sales are coming in and Kirsty continues to make all the products herself. There are plans for this to change in the future.

> *We really want to grow the business with the aim of getting our products manufactured. Being able to outsource production will allow us more time to concentrate on other areas of the business like sales, marketing and the brand.*

Watch this space as Luna on the Moon gets into its stride!

www.lunaonthemoon.co.uk

5. **Eventbrite (www.eventbrite.co.uk)** – a marketplace that sells neither products nor service but events! With Eventbrite, you can upload events, sell tickets, manage attendees and generate event reports. Attract new members to your community by tagging events with keywords, so they can be discovered by people searching the Eventbrite directory for events like yours (@eventbriteUK).

6. **Folksy (www.folksy.com)** – launched in the summer of 2008 by James Boardwell, Folksy has risen to become the most popular UK site for independently crafted and designed work and supplies. Folksy has a community of around 13,000 designers and makers, more than £1 million in sales annually, and over 250,000 visitors every month. To set up a Folksy shop, choose a brand name and have a banner and profile picture, or logo, ready to upload along with your first products to list (@folksy). (See the Angie Spurgeon Case Study in Chapter 4, which shows how Angie leveraged her Folksy shop to sell designs to large retailers.)

7. **iTunes (www.apple.com/itunes)** – if you are a creator of audio books, a publisher of podcasts or developer of apps, the iTunes platform is your route to market. Over 60 billion apps have been downloaded from the App Store, making it the world's largest mobile application platform. Become a registered Apple developer for the iPhone (**https://developer.apple.com/iphone**), submit audio books to iTunes via Audible, an Amazon.com subsidiary (**www.audible.com**) and create iBooks for the iPad through the iBookstore. Apple is opening up a world of opportunity for content creators and app developers (@itunes).

8. **iStock by Getty Images (www.istock.com)** – the web's original resource for crowd-sourced royalty-free stock images, media and design, offering millions of hand-picked photos, illustrations, videos and audio tracks. A site 'by creatives, for creatives', iStock began in 2000 as the pioneer micropayment photography site. Thousands of micro-stock photographers and videographers generate an income via the site through uploading work and selling to visiting customers. To sell on iStock you need to be a member. It is quick and free to join. You then have to take some online training and a quiz and upload samples of your work to be selected to sell on the site (@iStock).

Case Study

Name: Dean Mitchell

Business: Dean Mitchell Photography

Dean Mitchell started as a stock photographer in 2008 after 12 months spent carefully studying the microstock industry.

> *It appeared as though everything had already been done and to a very high standard by some contributors, but I could also see that people imagery was the most profitable stream of microstock photography. It was also highly changeable due to styles and trends, meaning there was an ever-increasing customer demand for new content. This was the space I wanted to get into!*

It was not until September 2008 that Dean decided to quit his full-time job to focus on shooting stock full time.

> *My wife was three months away from giving birth to our first child, I was earning low pay as a commercial photographer's assistant and I felt it was time to put all I'd learnt in to practice. At that time I couldn't rely solely on the earnings I got from iStock, as it was clear from my analytics that to sell stock images customers needed to see my work and that would be slow at the beginning with such a small portfolio. To subsidise that, I contributed to 15 microstock libraries and took on the odd commercial job here and there.*

> *Setting up an account with iStock was easy, but getting past strict inspection standards was tough. I look back now and smile because it taught me so much about setting a high standard in my work and also slowing down a little bit – even though I say it reluctantly, I would go as far as to say iStock has shaped me into a tiny bit of a perfectionist.*

With impressive results being generated from iStock, Dean reduced his distribution sites from fifteen to just one – that one being iStock.

I worked out that focusing on one marketplace would mean generating 100 per cent more income and my work would be seen four times more often. Everything changed for me in October 2011 when, after three years of crunching numbers, I decided to go exclusive with iStock. I now secure 83 per cent of my royalties from iStock and the remaining 17 per cent from iStock's parent company, Getty Images.

Dean suggests that by far the best way to increase and maintain sales is to know your distributor and what they want from you.

iStockalypse events are great for getting to know who's who, meet up or even collaborate with fellow contributors. The support I've received since attending these events has been fantastic.

http://deanmitchellphotography.com

9. **notonthehighstreet.com (www.notonthehighstreet.com)** – the site brings together small, creative businesses from across the UK and allows them to trade via one curated marketplace. Over 4,000 partners sell original and personalised crafted products that are promoted to over 27 million unique site visitors each year.

> *We look for businesses that have innovative and original ideas; something a bit different that are either designed or sourced by you. We also like to see great photography.*

To get started, complete a short online application format **www.notonthehighstreet.com/join/signup** and a new business team reviews your application to assess if your products are a good fit for this growing marketplace (@ notonthehighst).

10. **Amazon Marketplace (www.amazon.co.uk)** – Amazon has more than 21 million active customers in the UK. Have your

products promoted and sold to some of them! Sign up to Amazon Local to promote offers to potential customers in your area or sell on Amazon's European marketplaces using a single account. It is straightforward to upload inventory and using fulfilment by Amazon means the professionals take care of delivery, too (@AmazonUK).

11. **PeoplePerHour (www.peopleperhour.com)** – founded in 2007, this is an online marketplace connecting businesses with freelance workers and now home to more than 670,000 registered users in over 100 countries. By registering on the site, freelancers can showcase work and develop contacts with businesses keen to utilise their specialist skills.

> *Our typical users are skilled professionals who are full-time self-employed freelancers looking for new clients. We also have a pool of users who use the site to make extra money with their skills during evenings and weekends. Freelancers range in skills from copywriting and design to accounting and legal professionals.*

> *Small businesses are our typical service users. They don't want to hire full-time staff, they are time-poor and need to get their jobs done and fast. 87 per cent of small businesses who use the site go on to rehire the same freelancer they've used again.*

To get started, you can sign up in a few easy steps or simply import your LinkedIn profile (@PeoplePerHour).

12. **Yumbles (www.yumbles.com)** – launched by a husband and wife team who combined work experiences from online marketplaces with their love of food, to help fellow food lovers discover and buy independent, original foods online.

> *We're really proud to showcase a growing number of food and drink sellers from around the UK, including several Great Taste Award winners. Yumbles.com is already home to over 100 sellers with new shops launching every day – we individually approve applications to ensure the right fit and commitment to quality. Current sellers offer everything from organic chocolate to artisan seaweed, decadent sweets to high-quality spices.*

To sell with Yumbles, fill out a few details and apply online. With a thumbs-up from the team, it is easy to start selling and there is support available if you need it (@yumblesHQ).

Marketplace pricing

Here is what you can expect to pay to sell on the profiled marketplaces.

Marketplace	Cost
eBay **www.ebay.co.uk**	The fees are determined by what you sell, how you set up listings and whether you open a shop. Get started on the no fixed fee package, which entitles you to list up to 65 listings per month and pay commission of 8 to 11 per cent, depending on the category. **http://sellercentre.ebay.co.uk/ fees-business-sellers-0**
Elance **www.elance.com**	Free to join and you, as the freelancer, pay an 8.75 per cent service fee to Elance out of the payment you receive from clients. **http://help.elance.com/ entries/20216941-How-does-Elance-work-and-how-much-does-it-cost-**
Enterprise Nation **www. enterprisenation. com**	Free to create a profile and secure new opportunities from small businesses finding you on the marketplace.
Etsy **www.etsy.com**	You pay $0.20 to list an item on Etsy for four months, or until it sells. Once you sell your item, you pay a 3.5 per cent fee on the sale price.
Eventbrite **www.eventbrite. co.uk**	It is free to upload events and, if you aren't charging for tickets, there are no fees to pay. For every ticket that has a sales price, there is a charge of 2.5 per cent of the ticket value plus £0.65 per ticket, payable as fees to Eventbrite. **http://help.eventbrite.co.uk/customer/ en_gb/portal/articles/428604**

Folksy **www.folksy.com**	It costs £0.15 per item to list (excluding VAT) and each listing lasts for 120 days (four months approximately). When you make a sale you pay a 6 per cent commission. **https://folksy.uservoice.com/** **knowledgebase/articles/58077-how-** **much-does-it-cost-to-sell-on-folksy-**
iTunes **www.itunes.com**	For apps, Apple gives 70 per cent of revenues to the seller.
iStock **www.istock.com**	It is free to get started but you have to take some training, a quiz, and be selected as a seller. Once chosen, iStock sells your work and you receive a base royalty rate of 15 per cent for each file downloaded. If you are an Exclusive Contributor you can earn up to 45 per cent. **http://www.istockphoto.com/help/** **sell-stock/rate-schedule**
notonthehighstreet. **com** **www.** **notonthehighstreet.** **com**	There is a one-off joining fee to have your products appear on this marketplace and then a commission of 25 per cent per item sold.
Amazon **www.amazon.co.uk**	There are two pricing packages: Sell a little basic and Sell a lot PRO. With Sell a little basic, you can sell up to 35 products and pay only when you sell something. The commission – referred to by Amazon as a Closing Fee – is 15 per cent for books, music and video and from 7 per cent for all other categories. **http://services.amazon.co.uk/services/** **sell-online/pricing.html**
PeoplePerHour.com **www.** **peopleperhour.com**	Sellers are charged a 15 per cent service fee on the first £175 earned in a month and a service fee of 3.5 per cent (excl. VAT) on all work billed (earnings), above the first £175 earned in the month, which has a 15 per cent (excl. VAT) Service Fee.

Yumbles www.yumbles.com	Free to register and, for every sale, you pay £0.30 + 18 per cent (+VAT), e.g. if the sale value is £25, that is a charge of £4.80 (+VAT).

Template websites

Turn to template site providers to choose a template, upload products, complete descriptions and create a home on the web! It could not be more simple and most of the providers have free or low-cost starter packages.

Only a little technical expertise is required as you 'drag and drop' products and words into place. The beauty of opting for a template website is that the provider takes care of the technology and infrastructure, leaving you to focus on creating a great product or service, and attracting customers to buy.

Here are five of the more popular site builders and associated fees.

Site builder	Associated fees
Moonfruit www.moonfruit.com	Multiple options from free to £4 per month for the Lite package. The standard package for £8 per month offers the ability to upload 50 products to the shop, is mobile optimised and comes complete with a Facebook shop and Getty Images.
Shopify www.shopify.com	There is an option to start with a free 14-day trial. The Starter Plan is $14 per month, which allows you to sell up to 25 products and there is a 2 per cent transaction fee. The next package is $29 per month and offers unlimited upload of products.

Squarespace www.squarespace.com	A free 14-day trial followed by three packages starting at $8 per month to sell one product, $16 per month to sell up to 20 products or $24 per month to sell unlimited products.
Weebly www.weebly.com	The e-commerce package is $25 per month, which comes complete with a mobile store, inventory management and search engine optimisation built in.
Wix www.wix.com	Start a one-page website for free and upgrade to the e-commerce plan for £12 per month to start selling via your store.

Top tip

Register your company domain name and carry this name across to a blog or template website. Secure domains with the main registrars that also offer up to six months' free hosting include:

- GoDaddy: www.godaddy.com
- 1&1: www.1and1.com
- 123-reg: www.123-reg.co.uk

Your customers need YOU!

Regardless of the sales channel you use, consider the importance of creating a professional-looking online presence, as customers will make a decision in seconds as to whether they will buy from you. One of the first tabs they may click on is 'About us' – this section offers a great opportunity to tell your story and engage the customer with you, the business and the brand.

Customers will make a decision in seconds as to whether they will buy from you

What to include on this page:

- A top-quality image of you (see Chapter 7 for how to do this on a budget).
- The story of what encouraged you to start the business, how you came up with the idea, your values and motivations.
- If the family is involved and the business run from home, consider including images of this, too! Visitors immediately will feel connected to you and possibly that bit more likely to buy.

The following sites are particularly good when it comes to getting that 'About us' page just right:

- **Jimmy's Iced Coffee: http://jimmysicedcoffee.com**
- **Sarah J. Thomas Photography: http://sarahjthomas.com** (click 'The Video' tab, found under 'About')
- **Brandsonvine: www.brandsonvine.com**
- **English Bone China by Sara Smith: www.sarasmith.co.uk/ our-story.**

Capture customers in seconds by telling and showing your story on this page.

Top tip

Source free images for your website with Compfight (**compfight.com**), where images come free, so long as the photographer is attributed. Or look for credit deals with iStock by Getty Images (**www.istockphoto. com**). See Chapter 7 for a suggestion on how to source imagery for free across the business.

Offline sales

Meet customers face to face by selling at shows and markets, in pop-ups and shops. This route offers immediate customer feedback and the chance to capture data from potential customers. But how can you achieve this on a budget?

Trade shows

Look out for shows offering free space to start-ups. *Country Living* magazine runs an annual opportunity for 28 businesses to pop-up for free at its highly popular Spring Fair and, as the business looks to go global, consider UK Trade & Investment's Tradeshow Access Programme, offering financial support so you can show in new markets. Follow shows in your sector on Twitter and sign up to their newsletters to be the first to respond to opportunities and competitions to win free space.

Source: Shutterstock.com, © Graphic Store

Useful links include:

- Pop-up Market at the Country Living Spring Fair: www. countryliving.co.uk/kitchen-table-talent/ktt-events/ apply-for-our-2014-pop-up-market
- UK Trade & Investment Tradeshow Access Programme: www.gov.uk/tradeshow-access-programme.

Pop-up

Visit pop-up platforms Appear Here, PopUp Britain and We Are Pop Up to look for shops that ideally offer deals of no rent and a percentage of sales revenue, i.e. you do not pay for space, you pay a commission based on making sales. This is the arrangement in place at the Clerkenwell Collection run by the founders of one of the UK's fastest growing technology companies, Ve Interactive (**www.veinteractive.com**).

> *At the Clerkenwell Collection, we don't charge tenants up-front rent. Instead, we have a revenue-share agreement so, when the tenants make sales, we receive a commission. It incentivises tenants to do well and we all thrive together.*
>
> Kathy Heslop, Ve Interactive

Useful links include:

- Appear Here: www.appearhere.com
- PopUp Britain: www.popupbritain.com
- We Are Pop Up: www.wearepopup.com.

Shop share

A new model that is becoming popular on the platforms outlined above is shop share and it is a much more cost-effective route to get on the high street. Find a shop to share on these sites, or approach a shop yourself that you can see your customers visiting and promote the idea of you having a shelf or small space from which to sell. Pay the owner a commission on sales, as this means no upfront investment for you but you do start paying money as you start making money. For the shop owner, your products give customers an extra reason to come in and browse and you are an extra pair of hands to watch over the shop!

See Chapter 8 for advice on how to find your own space in which to host events, make sales or run the company.

These routes are well suited to businesses selling product. The same principles apply when selling services. Consider:

- speaking at events to demonstrate your expertise
- approaching potential partners who could offer your service in addition to their own. For example, if you start a business selling specialist financial services, could the local accountant benefit from promoting yours as an additional service to clients, in exchange for a revenue share?
- hosting an event to attract potential clients to you
- sending emails direct to potential clients (following the advice outlined above to make it personal, and be clear on the pitch) and follow-up calls/meet to secure a sale.

The following sections show how to host events, share expertise and meet with clients in a professional environment, without breaking the budget.

Complete this sales checklist to ensure that you are making the most of all commercial opportunities.

Online sales	Blog
	Marketplace
	Template site
Offline sales	Trade shows
	Pop-up
	Shop share
	Sales partnerships
	Direct sales

Total cost of making sales:

Online:	
Via blog	£0.00
Via marketplaces	£0.00 (only pay on making a sale)
Via template website	£0.00 (for content-only site or up to £25 for a month on a fully enabled e-commerce site)
Domain registration	£4.50
Offline:	
Shop share or pop-up based on commission	£0.00
Free space at trade shows	£0.00
Partnerships with complementary brands	£0.00
Meet with customer	£0.00
Total cost of online and offline:	£4.50

Total costs incurred to date:

Coming up with an idea	£0.00
Carrying out market research	£0.00
Writing a business plan	£0.00
Taking care of company admin	£20.00
Technology set-up	£2.50
Making sales	£4.50
Total:	£27.00

Chapter

7

Branding on a budget

It is now perfectly possible to become an expert, create a brand and get known, without having to spend a fortune. You will enjoy doing it and here is how to go about it.

A professional logo

Create a good first impression with a professional-looking logo. When it comes to where to turn to get help for this, look first to friends and family; do you know anyone who could design something for you to get the business up and running? Or consider a skill swap (see Chapter 9). The third option is to turn to websites on which millions of creative freelancers are awaiting your instruction. The benefit of using these sites is that you get lots of options presented from the freelancers pitching for work. I still remember returning from an event and receiving an email from someone who attended that day.

> On your suggestion, I went on to CrowdSPRING to get my logo designed. Four hours later, I've got 18 options from which to choose. I'm having so much fun!

Create a good first impression

The main platforms offer logos from $5 to $500. Here is what you can expect to pay.

Platform	Price for logo
Fiverr www.fiverr.com	As the name implies, $5!

▶

crowdSPRING www.crowdspring.com	Referring to itself as 'the world's leading marketplace for logos, graphic design and naming', prices for a logo start from $200.
99designs www.99designs.co.uk	A community of over 300,000 designers at the click of a mouse, prices start at £179.
PeoplePerHour www.peopleperhour.com	Freelancers quote various prices for logo design, starting from £20.
Elance www.elance.com	A search for logo design returns over 14,000 freelance options, with prices starting at $10.

With logo complete, upload this to your blog or website and onto hard copy promotion materials, such as business cards and flyers.

Business cards

An essential part of your start-up toolkit and something to be carried at all times, as you just never know who you might meet. Source business cards on a budget from companies such as:

- Vistaprint: www.vistaprint.co.uk – 100 cards for £9.99
- MOO: www.uk.moo.com– 50 cards for £10.99
- printed.com: www.printed.com – 100 cards for £12.83

Include on the cards key information that the recipient needs to know, such as:

- company name
- your name (if different from above)
- link to website
- link to social media
- telephone number.

Consider including your postal address, too. If starting the business at home, perhaps you do not want people to know this address for reasons of privacy or because you are keeping expensive kit or stock at home. In which case, consider a virtual office, which is where you rent an address. Post is sent either to that address for you to collect or you pay extra to have it sent on. Prices for a virtual office start at £38 per month from Mail Boxes Etc. (**www.mbe.co.uk**) or, if you are registered with an accountant, ask to use their mailing address for any written communication from HM Revenue & Customs.

Top tip

Consider a professional answering service, so calls are always picked up and clients get a friendly welcome. Moneypenny (**www.moneypenny.co.uk**) is a leader in this sector (we use them for Enterprise Nation calls) and they have introduced an app, Penelope, which allows small businesses to route calls to whichever number you are on, or to have them answered by a Moneypenny PA. Prices start from £21 per month, so something to consider when customer calls start coming in!

As the business builds sales, use extra budget to increase your print order and consider leaflets, flyers and postcards, too. These can be put on display at the trade shows, markets, pop-ups, shops and events covered in Chapter 6 Making sales.

With promotion cards and materials in hand, turn to social media and search engine optimisation to create a professional and powerful brand on the web, needing no investment but your time.

Social media

Social media has indeed been a friend of the small business owner and the five social media platforms profiled here give you the ability to reach customers, raise your profile and meet suppliers and partners, all for free.

Reach customers, raise your profile and meet suppliers and partners, all for free

Facebook

With more than 1 billion users across the globe and 30 million in the UK, a significant number of your present and potential customers spend time on Facebook every day. Create a Facebook Business Page and build an audience by inviting friends to share your page, and invite your business contacts, too. Visit Facebook's 'page insights' to look for trends so you can develop more of the best-performing and most engaging content. Visit **www. facebook.com/business** to get started.

Source: Shutterstock.com, © best works

Pinterest

Big brands and small businesses have taken to Pinterest to pin product pictures to virtual pinboards and to allow customers to pin those same products, so they become free marketing agents for you and the brand.

Pin things you think your users will find interesting and/or useful. Create a board of your products, employees, behind the scenes business action, fan photos, events, etc. Keep these pictures simple and visually appealing to increase the chances that they will be shared. Attract followers by following other people and link your Facebook and Twitter accounts to Pinterest. The more you use Pinterest, the more times your account appears, and so the more likely you will get a good following. There is plenty of research to show that people visiting your website or blog from Pinterest are more likely to buy, than traffic referred from any other social media platform, i.e. Pinterest users are often in the mood to shop!

Register a business account to get access to analytics to help you track activity and discover what pinners like. To get started visit **http://business.pinterest.com/en**

> ### Top tip
>
> With your audience in mind, think about the best time of day (or night!) to post to social media sites. If you are targeting the USA as a new market, tweet when they wake. Appealing to UK commuters? Tweet when they are commuting, etc.!

Twitter

Twitter has around 15 million active users in the UK and many more overseas. It is a powerful tool when it comes to sharing your expertise and reaching customers. A company I profiled a few years ago that was doing well selling overseas, said of Twitter and social media in general:

Social media has most definitely been our friend. We haven't paid for any direct advertising. We considered exhibitions but they are

> *expensive and with most of our international orders coming from Twitter and Facebook, which cost nothing, we're keen to continue and experiment more with social media marketing.*

Mark Shaw is an author who has written books for Enterprise Nation on how to make the most of Twitter and his advice is to tweet three types of messages: social chit-chat; the sharing of resources, links, tools, info, ideas and opinions; and tweets that answer questions that demonstrate your knowledge. I think this is a good menu to keep in mind.

Social media professional, Alison Battisby, suggests:

> *Twitter is a fantastic place for sharing interesting content and engaging in conversations with like-minded people. Think about your target customer, and reasons why they might be on Twitter. Share content that will interest them, and help to build your credibility.*
>
> *For example, if you are a hat company, share information about the latest trends in hats, inspiration about what kind of hats are good for which occasions, examples of celebrities wearing nice hats, and tell your customers the story behind your business and where you are selling your hats. Give your customers exclusive product news, special offers, the opportunity to feedback their thoughts and, from time to time, give them something for free!*

Find conversations to enter into via **search.twitter.com** and retweet (RT) other people's messages if they are of interest to you and your followers. Later on we look at how following journalists on Twitter and regularly checking the #journorequest hashtag can lead to profile and promotion. To get started visit **https:// business.twitter.com/en-gb**.

Top tip

If your start-up is selling in your own town or county, get involved in County Hours. From Cumbria to Colchester, these hours take place every day, and at different hours. Search for the area in which you are interested and join the conversation!

Case Study

Name: Sarah Hamilton

Business: Sarah Hamilton Prints

Sarah Hamilton is one business owner who has seen at first hand the benefits of using Twitter for business.

Twitter has made such an enormous difference to my business that I'd be here forever if I listed all the benefits! So, to be brief, I've made business connections with galleries I'd never even heard of and met other artists and designers who I've collaborated with. Aside from actual sales, which are hugely significant, I've also sourced suppliers, photographers and services. It has given me the scope to build my profile and I'm now a features writer at UK Handmade as a direct result of a Twitter meeting. Unleashing the amazing power of Twitter and social media should be a top priority to anyone starting a new business.

When it comes to advice on how to get it right, Sarah says:

Think strategically – don't simply chase sales. These come, but only after you build networks and relationships. Be generous, friendly and help other people, never be rude or antisocial, as this reflects badly on your business. Remember Twitter relationships take time to grow and nurture – as with most things,

> *a successful social media strategy is a long-term commitment.*
>
> With sales coming in from Twitter and elsewhere, Sarah is about to launch a studio range of home products and a new website and brochure to match.
>
> You can guarantee this entrepreneur will be posting company updates to Twitter!
>
> www.sarahhamiltonprints.com
>
> @SarahHamiltonPS

LinkedIn

Create a free profile on LinkedIn to be found by fellow professionals. With over 300 million people on this social network, it can, correctly, lay claim to being the world's largest rolling rolodex, and it is a particularly good site to be on if you are selling to corporate clients or big business.

A tool that I think particularly suits start-ups (and is free to use) is LinkedIn Groups. Create a group around your topic of interest and area of expertise and invite people to join. This is an effective way to find potential partners with common interest or future customers, keen to follow the conversation.

LinkedIn has a dedicated resource centre for small business showing how to use the platform for branding, marketing, making sales and hiring. See **http://smallbusiness.linkedin. com.**

Visit **www.linkedin.com** to get started.

Instagram

With over 75 million users, Instagram is a powerful and picture-filled route to market. Post images and have them liked, shared and commented on to gain social traction. Mallory Cravens is a student of entrepreneurship and offers five tips on how to make the most of this free tool.

1. **Create a story.** Showing in a series pictures that are related to one another provides your Instagram with a sense of continuity and progression. When all the pictures are random and independent of one another, the account can seem scattered, leading to brand confusion.

2. **Show different ways to use your product.** Supplying customers with useful information is helpful to them and gives them another reason to buy your product. Topshop does a good job of showcasing its products in helpful ways. It often posts videos on its Instagram instructing followers how to use its makeup line. New makeup trends can be intimidating and what better way to encourage people to try new things (your new things) than by showing them how to!

3. **Upload video.** A lot of celebrities post videos on their personal Instagram, but most businesses have yet to utilise this media. Mix it up with a video every now and then to keep your followers interested. Not only is it a way to promote your brand by creating mini commercials, but also by creating 'how to' videos, as mentioned above.

4. **Get personal.** Show pictures of your team, new hires and behind-the-scenes action. This allows people to see the personality and people behind your brand. If a customer posts a picture on their Instagram using your product – repost it and give them a shout out! A great way to connect with your customers on a personal level is to show them you are paying attention.

5. **Respond, respond, respond!** Always respond to your users' questions and tag them in your response. One of the perks of being a small business is that you can be closer to the customer. Show them you are committed by taking the time to comment back and make sure they see it, too.

Top tip

As well as Instagram, to promote your brand via voice and video, YouTube, Vine and Vimeo are other platforms of choice. Create content using your smartphone ▶

> and upgrade to hiring a professional videographer when there is money in the bank. Content could include vox pop testimonials from customers, a brief tour of the home office, footage of you making/selling/demonstrating your products. Experiment a little to test if this is how your market wants to engage.

Useful links include:

- **YouTube: www.youtube.com**
- **Vimeo: www.vimeo.com**
- **Vine: https://vine.co**

Jewellery maker Joanna Zhou learnt the skills for her business by watching YouTube videos. Now she has started her own channel that has become a business in its own right.

Case Study

Name: Joanna Zhou

Business: Maqaroon

I worked as a manga artist for many years and love everything related to kawaii culture. There's a crafting trend from Japan called Sweets Deco, which involves making accessories out of miniature fake food. After noticing how popular macaroons are at the moment, I was inspired to start a brand offering elegant sweets-deco jewellery designed for a European market.

Maqaroon launched in 2011 and it took a bit of time to develop a successful product. I had no experience designing jewellery so the early days were a steep learning curve. The brand in its current form has been going strong since early 2013 and the YouTube channel started in January 2014.

It was through watching YouTube tutorials when learning how to make sweets-deco jewellery that Joanna felt inspired to start her own channel.

> There's a genre on YouTube called ASMR (autonomous sensory meridian response), which are quiet videos designed to help people relax or fall asleep. My idea was to combine craft videos with ASMR because I hadn't seen anyone do this before.
>
> I make all the videos myself, although luckily I only need a very simple set-up because everything is filmed on a table-top area. I edit using iMovie, which I learned by watching a few tutorials on YouTube.

Joanna's channel is averaging 250,000 views per month with older videos still receiving consistent views and some heading towards 100,000.

> I didn't expect the channel to take off as fast as it did, so it's definitely becoming a business in its own right. I still get a high number of referrals to my online shop through YouTube, but I've stopped marketing products on the channel and instead I'm just focusing on creating good content for my audience.
>
> I was extremely surprised at how lucrative YouTube can be, and how underrated this business model is in the entrepreneurial or start-up scene. The website Socialblade.com provides relatively accurate estimates of channel growth and ad. revenue. So creating a business based on YouTube is far more reliable and predictable than a business plan for an untested product in any other market.
>
> A further advantage of YouTube is that it has extremely low overheads compared to a traditional business. A good channel becomes almost immediately profitable and revenue from older videos turns into a growing stream of passive income. There are teenagers all over the world making more profit from their

bedrooms than most start-ups manage within the first five years.

The hardest part is simply coming up with a concept that attracts subscribers and then maintaining the recommended minimum of one video per week to keep viewers engaged.

Joanna has ambitious plans for the development of the channel.

I would love to use it as a platform to inspire girls to develop their creative and business skills. I feel many people dismiss crafts as something fairly frivolous, but I believe that, on the contrary, crafts can be the best gateway into getting girls interested in business, branding and marketing. I've learned much more about marketing in the past two years of doing craft fairs than my whole career as a freelance designer before that. So I want to create a resource which combines tutorials and kawaii inspiration with solid design and business advice.

My goal is to share my experiences from running Maqaroon as a business with girls on YouTube so they can aspire to things beyond selfies, weight-loss and shopping. For instance, I filmed a video documenting my experiences at a trade show and that was the same event which led to Maqaroon being sold now in Harrods. These are insights that could change what girls thought was possible with their 'hobby', but they need to see someone doing it first to make it tangible.

www.maqaroon.com

www.youtube.com/maqaroon

People often ask me which one platform they should be on to reach customers. My response to this is: spend a little time exploring and uploading content to all the platforms, so you build a brand and become known across the web.

To enable this, turn to Hootsuite and TweetDeck as tools to save you time.

- **Hootsuite (https://hootsuite.com)** – outlined in the 'Software' section of Chapter 5, this is the tool to manage multiple social media accounts, schedule activity and measure results.

- **TweetDeck (https://tweetdeck.twitter.com)** – applicable only to Twitter, but with this tool you can manage multiple Twitter accounts, search effectively and schedule tweets.

Hayley Carr, aka London Beauty Queen (see the Case Study in Chapter 6), is all across the web and manages her social media workload through scheduling at the beginning of the week and responding throughout the week.

> *I've made it good practice to sit on a Monday morning and schedule the majority of my social content for the week, so there's at least something on every channel every day. However, most of the Twitter and all of the Instagram is me reacting to things as I go along. It's become second nature to be attached to my smartphone, so it's easy to keep my followers informed and interested.*

Track and measure what is working with tools like Google Analytics, Clicky and CrazyEgg and, based on the results, do more on the platform on which you are attracting most interest and engagement.

Useful links include:

- **Google Analytics: www.google.com/analytics**
- **Clicky: www.clicky.com**
- **Crazy Egg: www.crazyegg.com**
- **Social Blade: www.socialblade.com** (for YouTube analytics)

Dominic Sales is the founder of Gleam Futures, a business that manages the UK's top social talent, including Zoella, Tanya Burr and Lily Pebbles. These social stars have built followings of millions of people across the major media platforms. When I ask Dominic the secret to their success, he answers:

To become top social talent in the world you need to be dedicated, know how to make nice-looking, well-lit clear content, have the ability to take rejection and above all be real.

Enough said!

Search engine optimisation

Search engine optimisation (SEO) is the process you go through in order to be found on the web by suppliers, partners and customers. There are steps you can take – for free – to improve your SEO and appear higher in the search results when people are looking for what you offer.

The secret to getting SEO right comprises two main elements:

- producing fresh content, which appears across the web, and
- being on top of links.

Fresh content across the web

Produce fresh content for your website or blog as often as you can; ideally every day. This means that the search spiders that crawl the web looking for quality content are more likely to find and display you as the result when people are searching.

Produce fresh content for your website or blog as often as you can

Content can be blog posts, social media activity and/or video clips. Let us say you are in the business of delivering legal services for small businesses. You have a very good chance of appearing high in the results when people are searching for 'legal services for small business' if you are:

- blogging with top legal tips
- tweeting useful links to legal resources

- delivering online courses to small businesses on various legal topics via webinar tools or email software
- managing a legal LinkedIn group for small businesses
- developing an Instagram account with images related to law and small business
- quoted on other people's blogs as a small business legal specialist.

Start by writing and producing this content yourself and, as the business grows, consider outsourcing to others who are experts in content creation.

Link in and out

Inbound and outbound links to and from your site are also a route to attracting traffic.

If your business caters to local customers, get a listing on directories such as Google Maps (**https://maps.google.com**) and Bing Places for Business (**www.bingplaces.com**) in order to be found. The links that perform best are those from sites with high-quality content and traffic, such as the BBC. If you get covered in any national, local or trade news, ask the journalist if they will include a clickable link back to your site from the interview or feature.

Consider approaching the websites and blogs that your customers visit and offer to write guest posts for these sites; again kindly requesting a link back to your own site.

> **Top tip**
>
> Guest posts written by you should be practical and helpful, i.e. not too salesy! Give readers valuable information and they will be more likely to follow you, engage with you and interact.

Spending just an hour a day on producing and publishing content will reap rewards when it comes to people finding you more easily on the web. The easier it is to find you, the easier it is to buy from you!

The easier it is to find you, the easier it is to buy from you!

Get on the map!

Frank Vitetta is founder of Orchid Box and an expert in local SEO (**www.orchidbox.com**).

Users want, and now expect, to be able to find goods and services that are nearest to them wherever they are, and Google is providing them with exactly that. In 2011, 20 per cent of desktop queries had local intent and more than 53 per cent of mobile queries on Bing had local intent. These percentages are continually increasing.

List your site for free on these local directories to have more likelihood of being found:

- www.192.com
- www.yelp.co.uk
- www.scoot.co.uk
- www.hotfrog.co.uk
- www.cylex-uk.co.uk
- business.localmole.co.uk/
- www.localstore.co.uk.

As people get to hear about you and see you across the web, they will head for your site. Attract them back with email marketing.

Have a newsletter sign-up function clearly displayed on your blog or website to collect email addresses. When a visitor gives you their email address, they give you permission to keep them informed and to market yourself to them. With a daily updated list of email subscribers, send regular newsletters with company news, product launches, blog posts, upcoming events and other details you feel will interest this growing community.

Product	Price
MailChimp **www.mailchimp.com**	If you have fewer than 2,000 subscribers, you can send up to 12,000 emails per month for free.
Constant Contact **www.constantcontact.com**	A 60-day free trial is available. After that, the basic package is £15 per month for sending emails to up to 500 contacts.
Sign-Up.to **www.signupto.com**	Free for 30 days and then priced packages start from £19 per month.

Artist and entrepreneur Vera Blagev runs Vera Vera On The Wall and is about to test the value of a newsletter with her home-grown community.

Case Study

Name: Vera Blagev

Business: Vera Vera On The Wall

I knew I wanted to roll out a newsletter mainly because I read newsletters from other companies and artists but, with all this talk about social media, I wasn't sure if there was space for newsletters within people's limited attention span. It was reading A Crash Course in Email Marketing *that convinced me there is still a place for a newsletter, even in a social-media-dominated world.*

I have spent all summer adding more subscribers to my newsletter list as well as raising my profile on social media and my plan is to launch a first newsletter soon with subsequent newsletters going out every one to three weeks thereafter. In them, I'll include company

▶

> *news, product pictures, and competitions for special prizes or discounts. I plan to also include the occasional survey with specific questions to help me better understand my customers' preferences. It's all with a view to engaging with my audience and encouraging them back to the website.*
>
> www.veraveraonthewall.com

In a recent Enterprise Nation webinar, James Eder, founder of StudentBeans (**www.studentbeans.com**), which attracts millions of students to its website each month, gave his top tip for anyone wanting to create shareable content and a strong community:

Be relevant, engaging and useful.

I think this is good advice to follow when publishing content, growing a brand and promoting yourself across the web.

Offline promotion

Take the buzz that is developing online to the offline world. Appear in print and in person to give people yet more reason to talk about you and the brand. These moves can also be taken for free – you just have to be a little bit cheeky!

Meet the press

I have lost count of the number of times I have heard young start-ups say: 'It was a piece in the local newspaper/national press/on radio/TV that got us started in business.' Just one piece of positive press can be all you need to get a first order.

Just one piece of positive press can be all you need to get a first order

Editorial, which is the word to describe a journalist writing about you, is worth so much more than paid-for advertising. Readers, listeners, viewers consume the content (the same cannot be said for adverts!) and the feature will tell your story, as opposed to overtly selling to the consumer. Here are the steps to achieving that first bit of profile.

Identify journalists

Looking back at the market research in Chapter 2, if you have done this well, you will know your audience and, therefore, the publications reaching this audience. Head to a newsstand, record the names of the journalists writing in the papers and magazines that your customers read, and then search for their email addresses online. Follow them on Twitter (almost every journalist I know is now on Twitter), read their features and get to know the type of topics they cover and the style in which they write.

Know your story

Before making your approach, you have to understand your own brand. As Kiki Loizou, enterprise editor of *The Sunday Times*, puts it: 'If you don't know your story, how am I meant to tell it?' Have it clear in your own mind as to what you stand for and how you want to be spoken about and represented.

I referred to him before and return again to the story of Jimmy's Iced Coffee as, in my view, he has done a great job of crafting the story. This is how it goes:

- Jim goes to Australia in search of a better life.
- While there he discovers great-tasting cold coffee.
- Facing the reality of needing to return to the UK to get a job, he goes in search of cold coffee.
- He does not find anything he likes back in his homeland.
- He decides to partner up with his sister, Suze, to see if they can recreate a product for the UK market.

- The product (whose ingredients Jim describes oozing with passion) are placed in playful packaging and Jim and his sister set out on a fun and rewarding journey to sell their cool, cold coffee to major supermarkets, including Tesco, Waitrose and Ocado, and to WHSmith.

- Throughout this, they communicate with customers with daily tweets from the office and Instagrams from sales trips and events where they are dressed as coffee cartons.

The story is well-told, authentic and dynamite material for a journalist!

These are some of the points journalists look for in a story:

- Have you overcome the odds to start a business?

- Did you give up law to go into leotards, move from the City to making cupcakes? (Anything that offers an angle of before and after, which are very different, is very good!)

- How are you standing out? Selling in a different way, going into new markets, revolutionising the way we currently buy as consumers?

- Can it be connected with something current? Meat scandal at the supermarkets? Witness a rise in stories on handmade and artisanal food producers – make the most of these opportunities when they occur.

Small Business Saturday attracts the headlines

Leverage national campaigns like Small Business Saturday (**www.smallbusinesssaturdayuk.com**) to get your message across. Now in its second year, this one-day event, hosted in December, encourages consumers across the UK to shop at small businesses on the day. In the lead up, and on the day itself, media will look for stories of small business retailers. Make yourself known to the campaign, or direct to media, and be one of them. It is a free profile for you and boosts a national effort to increase sales for small businesses.

Other national campaigns include:

- **Global Entrepreneurship Week** (November): **www.gew.co**
- **Independent Retailer Month** (July): **www. independentretailermonth.co.uk**
- **Buy British Day** (October): **www.bestofbritannia.com/tag/ buy-british-day**
- **Made in Britain** (year-round): **www.madeingb.org**.

> **Top tip**
>
> Contact Enterprise Nation with your story! Across our campaigns, website and events, we are always profiling start-ups and growing businesses and we love a good small business story! Make contact via hello@ enterprisenation.com so we can add to your media clippings, too.

These campaigns give you, the start-up, an opportunity to tie your story into a national event and movement.

Make contact

With your story clear, and confidence intact, it is time to contact the journalists. If the journalist writes for a Sunday paper, go for contact at the beginning of the week and, if it is a monthly magazine, be aware that the editorial team is working on editions months in advance. After sending a first email, if there is no response, politely follow up with a second. What you are aiming for in this first contact is to make the journalist stop and think, 'I could use this'. Help them by sending:

- a release or media note
- quantifiable stats
- quotes from you and spokespeople/celebrities/others
- images in low resolution format

- reference to any awards/credentials you have
- a media contact (most likely, you!) who can help with more detail, if required.

Let us take an example.

> **Top tip**
>
> Search the #journorequest hashtag on Twitter to see if journalists are searching for a case study that sounds like you.

Student launches start-up blog to help young entrepreneurs realise their dreams

These are the key points to include in the release:

- The background of the start-up owner and what has driven/ motivated them to start this blog.
- The source for the statistic showing that 65 per cent of young people now say they would rather become their own boss than get a job.
- Quote from an official spokesperson saying that this comes at a time when the Government has just released a report to encourage youth entrepreneurship.
- Start-up owner sets out the vision for the company.
- A testimonial of a happy customer.
- A link where the journalist can go to find out more.

Keep in touch

If at first the journalist does not use your release, do not give up! Keep in casual contact, letting the journalist know, via email or social media, what the key milestones of the business are so, when they come to write a piece on young people starting online businesses, you are the person in their mind.

Be available

What you are after is to become the go-to person for a journalist. When that happens, drop everything else to return their call, offer the quote, write the opinion piece, etc. You may not get a second chance!

Become the go-to person for a journalist

Become an Enterprise Nation member and get a free PR consultation with our own head of media, Liz Slee, who, in one glance, can pick up the most PR-worthy parts of your business.

> **Top tip**
>
> **A picture says a thousand words**
>
> Have professional imagery to hand to send with a release or on request. How do you do this on a budget? Approach your local college and head for the photography department. Ask students if they would like to take pictures of you and the business, in exchange for using them in their portfolio.

Host events

Putting on events can be done on a shoestring budget, yet generate decent return in the form of profile and sales. Approach someone who has a space that would be ideal for the event and an owner who wants the kind of footfall you can attract. Give the event a hook with a speaker (who has a relevant message for your audience) and free refreshment! Approach food and drink suppliers who, again, would like access to your audience and ask if they might cater for free or at a heavy discount. This is where the principle of beg, borrow and barter kicks in again!

Philip Crilly is a fine example when I think of start-ups hosting an event on a budget, while still making a memorable first impression.

A pharmacist by day, Philip attended an Enterprise Nation event with his idea for gluten-free granola. He left by offering to blog for us, over 12 weeks, on his start-up journey. The blog series duly appeared and proved popular. Philip decided to contact Greg Wallace of Masterchef fame to share the blog series and ask if they could meet. Not only did they meet, Greg also agreed to let Philip use his restaurant for the Eatibbles product launch. For a start-up on a budget, that was quite some launch!

Host competitions

Create a buzz by running competitions. This could be to win one of your products or services, which you could run through any of the social media platforms or by using online form, Wufoo, outlined in Chapter 2. Or present your product as a prize to an influential blogger so they run the competition on their blog, reaching out to their readership as well as yours. Tap into national celebration days to make the most of the promotion aspect. At Enterprise Nation we run an offer on books on National Book Day and Summer Sales on Bank Holidays. These promotions are shared with a receptive audience and you can grow your audience by tapping into hashtags on Twitter connected to the cause.

Enter awards

Raise profile and earn prizes by entering awards. Some of them come with hard cash as the prize, which is most welcome when starting on a budget. Follow the tips outlined below.

Top tip

For entering (and winning) awards

1. **Eyes and ears open.** New awards and categories for small business are launched regularly. We have seen recently the introduction of the Duke of York New Entrepreneur of the Year Award and Enterprise Nation's own Top 50 Advisers Awards. They join others such as the Startups Awards, Smarta 100 Awards and

---

The Pitch. Be on Twitter, Facebook and a frequent visitor to the small business blogs, listed in Chapter 6, to stay tuned to award opportunities and deadline dates.

2. **Produce a winning entry.** Tell your story in the entry and bring it to life with top-quality imagery. Kate Edmunds is founder of creative gift and greeting cards business Eggnogg, and recently won an award in the Supreme Innovation & Design Awards. Kate's advice is: 'Enter a unique product that you're passionate about accompanied by a well-written piece about you and your product and good photography is essential. Your entry will shine through!'

Consider getting help with the wording from a professional copywriter or PR professional. Finally, it sounds obvious, but submit your entry within the deadline date!

3. **Perfect the pitch.** If you are shortlisted, and this involves presenting to judges, here are a few tips: practise, practise, practise the pitch; drink water and breathe before you go in; do the pitch standing up (you will come across as more confident and optimistic); and, if you are pitching a product that is portable, bring samples to leave for the judges. This is not bribery – you are purely trying to stand out and leave with a good impression!

If the award is to recognise the business, be sure to prepare for questions on everything from finances to growth plans and how you would make the most of winning the award. Organisations running awards want to know that you will promote a successful result, too. If winners are to be announced at an awards dinner, be sure to show up!

4. **Promote.** If you win the award, tell everyone you know! Write a release, contact the local press/radio/TV and display your win on the website, email sign-off and, if relevant, company promotion materials. You want

> customers, suppliers and the media to know that you are a winning company that takes innovation, customer service, product design, etc. seriously.
>
> 5. **Persist.** Maybe for this award, your application was not successful. In which case, keep trying! Different awards look for different attributes in a business. If at first you do not succeed, do not give up. You will find the judges and award-giving body that see the brilliance in your operation, and want to celebrate and recognise this so others can be inspired.

At the end of the day, every small business owner is a winner. Find the award that recognises you as such!

Agree to speak

If you are asked to speak at an event in your sector or industry, reply with a resounding yes! As with sales, not everyone enjoys public speaking, but the benefits outweigh your doubts; you just never know who might be in the audience or, indeed, on the same panel. I once asked a young milliner to speak at a fashion event we were hosting. It took some persuading for her to say yes. On the day, she was on the same panel as the chief executive of Harvey Nichols. They met and this led to a pitch to the buyers of this exclusive store. Be open to the opportunity and who knows where it will lead!

> **Top tip**
>
> When speaking in public, be clear in your mind what you want to say; have a beginning, middle and end and treat the talk as a conversation. Throughout your talk, remember to pause and breathe!

Hire a celebrity!

Encourage celebrities to say nice things about you, your product or service and be seen instantly by, potentially, millions of people. One company that has done this supremely well is Gandys Flip Flops. Brothers Rob and Paul Forkan started the business after a personal disaster when they were orphaned in the Sri Lankan tsunami. Their company produces flip flops with profits going towards building orphanages and they have managed to get their product in the hands of stars who have tweeted, blogged and Instagramed their feet in them. Cofounder Rob recently presented at one of our events and showed tweets from Jessie J, messages of support from Richard Branson and endorsements from British Prime Minister, David Cameron. Not bad for a young business on a budget, with the ambition to give it a go.

Big budgets

Big companies are keen for you to be the story and what this means is free promotion. Global costume company Morphsuits (**www.morphsuits.co.uk**) benefited from taking the star lead in a TV advertisement produced by international sourcing platform Alibaba (**www.alibaba.com**). In addition, online insurance provider Simply Business (**www.simplybusiness.co.uk**) recently ran a competition offering 12 companies the opportunity of free billboard advertising, with accounting software provider, Sage, running a similar 'Bag yourself a billboard' campaign, offering one young business a free 160-square-metre billboard in the heart of Tech City in London. Tune in to social media to look out for these competitions and opportunities and see Part 4 for more ways in which big business can lend a helping hand.

By recommendation

The ultimate promotion that any start-up or growing business seeks to achieve is word of mouth or, in the online world, word of mouse recommendation. This is when your existing customers and fans rave about you, so encouraging their own network to take a look too. The reason it is so valuable is because people buy based on what their friends, family and peers recommend and if they are recommending you, this constitutes free marketing and a powerful sales channel.

The ultimate promotion is word of mouth

Encourage it through:

- **Refer a friend programme** – incentivise customers to introduce their network. This could be through a discount, e.g. '£5 off your next purchase when you refer a friend' or an added extra, e.g. 'Get the deluxe for the price of the standard when you refer a friend'.

- **Customer testimonials** – upload pictures, quotes and even short video clips of your customers saying nice things about your business. Remember to ask the customer's permission before going public!

- **Social sharing** – add social share buttons to your website or blog to make it effortless for visitors to spread the word. Use AddThis (**www.addthis.com**) to add all the major social media platforms.

Attract customers, visitors, followers and fans through online and traditional media and you will soon be the start-up that everyone is talking about.

Total costs of branding on a budget:

Logo	£3.30 ($5.00)
Business cards	£9.99
Social media	£0.00
SEO	£0.00
Email marketing	£0.00
PR	£0.00
Events, competitions, awards	£0.00
Total:	**£13.29**

Total costs incurred to date:

Coming up with an idea	£0.00
Carrying out market research	£0.00
Writing a business plan	£0.00
Taking care of company admin	£20.00
Technology set-up	£2.50
Making sales	£4.50
Branding on a budget	£13.29
Total:	£40.29

Part

4

Going for growth

Sales are coming in, you are getting known and customers are returning for more of what you have to offer. Get the business ready for growth with creative space, expert support and an injection of funds. This section points you in the direction of all the resources a growing start-up needs.

Chapter

8

Finding space

As outlined in Chapter 4, I highly recommend you start the business from home to keep costs and commuting time as low as possible. This leads to a requirement for space both inside the house, and out, and multi-functional space, too. When starting out, you may need space from which to work, make sales, have meetings and collaborate. In this chapter, I offer a spacious range of options.

The home office

If you can, find dedicated space in the house from which to work. That way, you can close the door at the end of the working day and feel a physical sense of separation between what is work and what is not. Shoo Rayner is a children's author and illustrator and works out of a garden office. It is something he recommends to others.

> *Try to work in a shed or outhouse, or at least a dedicated room, and tell everyone that, when you're in there, you are at work so they should leave you alone. Ignore all attempts to draw you out – they will soon get the message!*

At the outset, when budget is tight, the main pieces of furniture you need in the home office are a robust desk and chair. Jeff Bezos, the founder of Amazon, famously used an old door as his desk when he started the company from his garage in Seattle. Asked about the desks in an interview in 1998, the now billionaire explained:

These desks serve as a symbol of frugality and a way of thinking. It's very important at Amazon.com to make sure that we're spending money on things that matter to customers.

Back to your home office; the best way to keep costs low is to use furniture you already have but, if you would rather buy new items, there are deals to be had. Look online at IKEA, B&Q and John Lewis for the keenest prices or visit recycling community site, Freecycle (**www.freecycle.org**), to find a piece of furniture that you want and someone else no longer does.

A final touch to your home office in the early days and, indeed, as the business grows, is a vision board. This could be a virtual vision board, using a platform like Pinterest, or get a basic cork board, for as little as £2, and stick to it images of what you want to achieve in the business, and in life. It could be places you want to visit, targets for the business, maybe even people you want to hire! Pin them on the board and this will be your daily reminder of what you are working towards.

Corby Kuffor is a young entrepreneur running ThatSaleSite (**thatsalesite.com**) from his bedroom in the family home:

Starting a successful business from home is extremely convenient, but also distracting, with your TV, games console and bed within touching distance. So I advise to always keep your business goals and ambitions at an even closer distance, as these are the things that will keep you focused and determined to work hard towards success.

Space outside the home office

Head outside the home office to work in third spaces, co-working hubs, hotel lobbies or just about anywhere else with free Wi-Fi!

Of the thousands of home business owners I have met over the years, they all comment on how much they enjoy working from home, but the one challenge can be a sense of isolation; missing the water cooler moment of an office and not having anyone with whom to bounce ideas around. Achieve this, and more, from the list of locations on the following pages. Simon Jenner, whose Urban Coffee Emporiums Case Study follows shortly in this chapter, tells me two start-ups met at one of his hosted MeetUps and went on to marry. Working out of the home office may get you more than you bargain for!

Coffee shops have become a popular stomping ground for start-ups

Local library

In Chapter 2 I covered the benefits of visiting the Business & IP Centres in major libraries in your closest city centre. At them, you will find access to IT equipment and free Wi-Fi. Head to your local library to find a quiet work environment, free desk space and business books on tap.

Enter your postcode in the Department for Communities and Local Government website to find the library closest to you: **www.gov.uk/local-library-services.**

Coffee shops

Known as 'the third space', which is neither office nor home, coffee shops have become a popular stomping ground for start-ups. Laden with available sockets, all-day supply of whatever takes your fancy, and perfect perches for people-watching, no wonder the coffee shop is one of the preferred workspaces of the sociable start-up!

Simon Jenner is the entrepreneur behind Urban Coffee, which started with one store, known as an Emporium, in Birmingham, and has now expanded to four locations that have become the meeting place for local start-ups and entrepreneurs.

Case Study

Name: Simon Jenner

Business: Urban Coffee Company

Simon Jenner had always loved coffee and, in 2009, while sitting with his business partner in a great independent coffee shop in London, questioned why he could not get similarly great coffee outside of London.

That was the eureka moment. Prior to Urban we were both working in IT, so knew nothing about coffee or retail. How hard can it be?

Urban Coffee has become successful and well-known on the back of its great coffee and on account of offering free space to start-ups wanting to host meet-ups and events.

In our business plan, we saw events and meet-ups as a key and a significant revenue generator, but the reality has been very different. People who come to meet-ups often don't buy anything and therefore it often costs us more in staff wages to stay open late. However, we think it acts as a great marketing activity and really enjoy being at the heart of all these weird and wacky events.

These events are now happening across Birmingham and Coventry as Urban Coffee has expanded and continues to attract an entrepreneurial following.

We see each Emporium as being the urban equivalent of the village hall and we want lots of activity going on. I guess because we made it free and open to any meet-ups, it was likely to attract entrepreneurs, the free Wi-Fi helped as well. The key ingredients to attract entrepreneurs are good coffee, free open Wi-Fi, big tables they can work at, a relaxed environment and interesting stuff going on.

As the business continues to look for new locations, the founders are influenced by the demographics of a location and number of start-ups resident in it.

> Our Jewellery Quarter Emporium has a good number of start-ups around it that regularly use it and we knew they were craving good coffee. After all, most start-ups are built on coffee!

www.urbancoffee.co.uk

@urbancoffeeco

Have a friendly local coffee shop to use as your 'meeting room' – it's much better than inviting clients to come round for a coffee when the washing machine is on!

Oliver Bridge, founder, Cornerstone

Top tip

View the WorkSnug video on 'Coffee Shop Etiquette for Mobile Workers' to be sure of working without disturbing! **http://blog.worksnug.com/2014/07/15/video-coffee-shop-etiquette-for-mobile-workers/**

Hotel lobbies

Rapidly filling with start-ups making their pitch, hotel lobbies, as with coffee shops with their free Wi-Fi and caffeine on call, present you with a professional space in which to meet clients and a home from home to get work done.

Shopping centres

Admittedly, not the first place you think of when thinking of where to go and work on your business, but shopping centre groups are increasingly looking to attract entrepreneurial footfall; as tenants in their malls and shoppers on the floor. For this reason, this is another place where you are likely to find free Wi-Fi and table space to touch down and polish up the business plan. See 'Space to sell' later on in this chapter for details of a competition run by one of the largest shopping-centre operators, offering start-ups free space from which to trade.

Co-working spaces

As the number of people starting a business has risen, so have the number of workspaces, too. There are national serviced office providers, of which Regus is the largest, and local hubs, so you can head out of the home office to work alongside others – and share resources.

The following table lists four options with the widest networks.

Company	Package
Regus **www.regus.co.uk**	The largest office provider of them all, Regus has 2,000 locations in 750 cities across 100 countries so, if your start-up needs space in the UK, or anywhere else for that matter, this could be your solution. Get a BusinessWorld card for £35 per month and get access to business lounges, free Wi-Fi and refreshments and discounts on meeting rooms. Buying a 12-month BusinessWorld contract comes with the first month free.
Bizspace **www.bizspace.co.uk**	Over 100 sites in England and Scotland offer co-working space, meeting rooms and grow-on space. Rent space from £3 per hour or around £20 per day.

Club Workspace http://www.workspace.co.uk/co-working-and-shared-office-space	Club Workspace is the co-working arm of Workspace Group, a publicly listed company with millions of square feet of office and commercial space in London. Choose from eight co-working centres and three price packages starting from £200 per month for three days per week access to £300 per month for a dedicated desk.
National Enterprise Network http://www.nationalenterprisenetwork.org	A network of Enterprise Agencies that cover 90 per cent of the country. Many of the agencies manage their own workspace, so can offer space alongside business support. Search the directory to find your nearest agency.

Regus Express

Seeing that start-ups wanted to work on the move, serviced office operator Regus formed a whole new division called RegusExpress, which is seeing office space popping up in service stations and Staples stores across the UK. Complete an online form to get a free one-day pass (**www.regus.co.uk/express**).

Hubs and co-working spaces are coming to life in local areas, too. The following entrepreneurs in Calder Valley and Farnham took matters into their own hands and started hubs in their areas to accommodate a rise in the number of start-ups looking for a desk and a place to connect.

> ## Case Study
>
> ### Business: Made in the Valley
>
> Made in the Valley is a cooperative of makers in the Calder Valley of West Yorkshire. With a building identified as a potential co-working and maker space, four entrepreneurial women came together to raise funds to heat the space and create a conducive work environment.
>
> *We're a group of four designer-makers based in the beautiful Calder Valley of West Yorkshire. Katch, Rachel and Amy all have degrees in Art and Design and Sue, a generation older, helps out. For several years now we've patiently persisted in producing and selling lovely textiles, ceramics, prints and artwork at the same time as working day jobs to pay the bills. It's hard competing with the work of many other talented makers in a crowded marketplace, not to mention mass-produced goods. You have to be good at, or at least competent in, so many areas – book keeping, marketing, selling, negotiating, the list goes on. We've learnt that doing things together is the way forward, so we've organised pop-up shops, run workshops and started to develop our own small range of sewing kits. Last year we organised an interactive Meet the Makers Market as part of the South Pennines Making and Doing Festival. We brought in small food producers and community businesses, as well as designer makers, and stall holders had to demonstrate their process and share their skills in some way with the customers. It was a great success and gave us the chance to tell the small business story. This year we got serious. We set up as a cooperative consortium to build on what we've already achieved.*
>
> *We needed a bigger home and more facilities to keep going, so we went hunting for commercial property. We've found a factory that has been empty for years,*

easy walking distance from the town of Hebden Bridge with plenty of parking, in a quiet industrial area next to beautiful woods, fields and a river. At the same time, we discovered co-working and saw a business opportunity – we could share our good fortune! We talked about it on Twitter and Facebook and in our small town and circulated a questionnaire.

We've gathered a group of enthusiastic potential subscribers – as well as other makers we've got gardeners, community businesses, graphic designers, advice workers and many others expressing an interest and a need. We're planning to offer screenprinting, photographic and sewing facilities and a tool library; space for meetings, workshops, packing, storage; office and kitchen facilities; support and advice for start-ups; opportunities to meet collaborators and make business contacts; joint marketing and selling events; and mutual support and friendship. Subscribers will be able to rent space daily, one or a few days a week or full time. We have prepared extensive figures and cash flow forecasts but we know that we need to stay flexible and respond to the needs of our customers. We have some funds from family and friends and we're planning a crowd-funding campaign, but we know we'll have to bootstrap this business and grow bit by bit.

At the moment our space is big and empty and we think it's beautiful. We'll make it even more beautiful, so that people will want to come and work here.

www.madeinthevalleyshop.co.uk

@madeinthevalley

Emma Selby had been running businesses from her own home before winning a building in a competition that has become a honey pot for Farnham's entrepreneurial community.

Case Study

Name: Emma Selby

Business: The Farnham Hub

I was a freelance bookkeeper at the time of setting up the Hub, although I previously ran a sports underwear business from home (fun fabric tennis knickers and riding bras). I sold the business when I had little ones and it got too much –and when there was no Hub to connect me to support!

The Hub evolved from a previous incarnation called ThinkingBus. ThinkingBus was a weekly co-working morning and creche for business mums in a local hotel, something I had been thinking about starting since I was mum of two young children running the underwear business. I got some sponsorship from our local media mogul Sir Ray Tindle to conduct some market research, found business owners wanted their skills updating and started doing that on a weekly basis, too. Men started to arrive – we now have more men than women on board – and I persuaded experienced entrepreneurs to deliver the training in return for a stream of potential customers. Now we have 120 members and a co-working and training premises open six days a week.

Emma secured the premises by winning it in a business competition!

A garden centre was opening a massive retail space and the operator was looking for a local business to bring in extra footfall. The space is a self-contained room within a busy garden centre on the A325 between Farnham and Bordon.

At the Hub we offer workshops, networking, co-working and training as well as business advice and signposting. We have different membership plans for 'innovators' 'collaborators' and 'contributors'.

Monthly memberships range from £50 to £200 and we offer an innovative training programme for entrepreneurs and their teams called 'Hub U' as well as the networking and co-working events. All our members can access business services and admin support at the Hub too.

The plan is to establish the Farnham Hub as a profit-making model and then replicate it and scale. There are home businesses in every town and they all need a Hub!

www.businesshubs.org

@thefarnhamhub

Space for growth

Apply to rent government office space for free. The Government has made available spaces including offices, workshops, retail and laboratory space that come with workstations, Wi-Fi and meeting rooms and are located across the UK. There are over 1,000 desk spaces available in total. The only cost to pay is £25 for a security check (**www.gov.uk/rent-government-workspace**).

> ## City space
>
> Visit the 3Space website to find free office space in London. This company takes on space that is empty on a temporary basis, and lets small businesses move in for free. The only downside? You have to leave when the landlord says, 'Time's up!' (**http://3space.org**).
>
> For Birmingham start-ups, there is free space on offer from local company, Time etc, that comes complete with commercial connections (**http://space.timeetc.com**).

Space to make

There is good news for the growing community of makers and designers as space opens for you, too! If starting a business requires access to specialist equipment like 3D printers or precision equipment machinery, others are making the investment so you do not have to. Search for maker spaces where equipment can be rented by the hour and there are specialist services on hand. Here are five across the UK.

Name	Offer
Building BloQs **www.** **buildingbloqs.** **com**	'Empowering makers and artists to invent and innovate' is the line from this makerspace in North London, which offers access to bench space, wood work and metal work for a membership fee of £20 per month.
FabLab **Manchester** **www.** **fablabmanchester.** **org**	An idea that started in the USA, the UK's first FabLab to open was in Manchester in 2010, set up to 'inspire people and entrepreneurs to turn their ideas into new products and prototypes by giving access to a range of advanced digital manufacturing technology'. Free to use on open Public Days with a pay-as-you-go system to prototype products.

	Owned by the Manufacturing Institute, a foundation has been formed to promote the Fab Lab concept across the UK and develop a network of 30 facilities with over 30,000 users by 2020.
Maker Space www.makerspace. org.uk	A community-owned and run workshop in Newcastle Upon Tyne with membership starting from £10 per month.
Makerversity www.makerversity. org	Based at the beautiful and historic Somerset House, this is a making and learning space, providing affordable and accessible space for makers.
London Hackspace https://london. hackspace.org.uk/	A not-for-profit member organisation with space and machinery in Hackney, open to members who pay what they can afford for membership.

Space to sell

Find space to sell through entering competitions, approaching potential partners and generally being innovative in thinking about where your customers are gathering and how you can get in front of them, at no cost to the business. A competition to help start-up traders get to market is Retail Factor, which has proven a success for both the organisers and the winners.

Top tip

Are you aged 16 to 25 and do you want somewhere to host a launch, put on a fashion show, run a focus group? Check out **www.somewhereto.com**, which offers free options for young people looking for space.

One of my favourite businesses that I have profiled and followed from the start is Arianna Cadwallader of Saturday Sewing Session. Wanting to start a sewing class in her area of North

London, Arianna had the vision but no budget. She approached the landlord of her local pub and asked to use the first floor of the pub, for free, on a Saturday morning, in exchange for bringing in people who would buy drinks on a floor that normally sat silent. He agreed, Arianna started her business, and now has a dedicated studio from which classes are run each day.

Without that free space when I started out, I'd never have got going. My advice to anyone needing space is to find the kind of space you're after, see when it's quiet, and ask the person who owns it if you can use it during that quiet time, in exchange for a benefit to them. If you don't ask the question, you'll just never know!

Competition name: Retail Factor

Host organisation: The Mall and Capital & Regional

The Mall launched Retail Factor nine years ago. We recognise that our success relies on the vibrancy of the surrounding town centre and the local community. The idea was to create a business competition that would offer local businesses the chance to test their business model and get a real taste of what the retail environment is like by trading for free in The Mall. Over 500 businesses have entered the competition since it launched and, every year, 10–15 start-ups get an opportunity to trade for free in the malls.

Historically, we focused on start-up businesses, but, with the growth of online retail, we see more and more online businesses wanting to test their offer in the physical retail environment, so we are now encouraging online businesses to apply. In the past, we ran the competition on Retail Merchandising Units, which are the kiosks you see in the malls and outside the shops but, this year, we trialled 'share a shop' in some locations and it worked really well for us and

> *the participants. We are continually looking at ways to improve the competition to open up access to even more start-ups.*
>
> Anna Steyn, Capital & Regional

Space to collaborate

A common thread throughout this book is the appetite that big businesses have to open up their assets to start-ups. One of the ways in which they are doing this is by offering accelerator space. Here are four London-based accelerators, backed by big business that are free for you, the start-up, to access.

Accelerator	Backed by
WAYRA **www.wayra.org/** **en**	Telefónica If chosen to enter WAYRA, you receive six months' space, mentoring support, up to €50,000 and access to the Telefónica customer base.
IDEALondon **www.idea-** **london.co.uk**	Cisco, DC Thomson and UCL look for the brightest of digital companies. On entering the accelerator, you receive space, mentoring and introductions to corporate partners of the hosts.
The Bakery **www.** **thebakerylondon.** **com**	Backed by brands including Unilever, BMW, Panasonic and Heinz. Brands come to the Bakery to find products and services to take to market. One of them could be yours!
TrueStart **www.truestart.** **co.uk**	Accenture, Land Securities and White & Case are partners in this accelerator focused on retail technology start-ups. Benefit from six months of space, up to £50,000 in investment and business services to the value of £75,000.

If an accelerator is not quite what you are after, consider approaching large corporates to ask about access to other kinds of space. If there is one thing that big business has by the bucket load, it is space! Approach with suggestions like these:

- You working from their office, in exchange for sharing your entrepreneurial energy.
- You hosting events onsite, with your job being to attract a crowd of the type the big business is after.
- You selling from a new development and filling a temporary gap, as the landowner finds a full-time tenant, etc.

Find what you are after on the Enterprise Nation Opportunities channel **(www.enterprisenation.com/opportunities)**, where large corporates are profiling the assets they have that are on offer to you.

Whatever the space requirement, you will find it on a budget by looking out for deals, competitions and promotions and approaching those with space to ask if you can use it, in return for tangible benefit. You have just got to beg, borrow and barter!

You have just got to beg, borrow and barter!

Total costs of space:

Home office	£20.00 (fixtures and furnishings)
Out of home work/trading space	£0.00
Total:	£20.00

Total costs incurred to date:

Coming up with an idea	£0.00
Carrying out market research	£0.00
Writing a business plan	£0.00
Taking care of company admin	£20.00
Technology set-up	£2.50
Making sales	£4.50
Branding on a budget	£13.29
Finding space	£20.00
Total:	£60.29

Chapter

9

Hiring people

When starting out in business, and indeed when continuing to grow, surround yourself with supportive people. People who will motivate, mentor and offer the practical and hands-on help you need to succeed. It is perfectly possible to achieve on a budget. Here is where and how to find them.

Find the person who will spur you on

The motivator

No need to stray far from home for this one. This could be your mum, spouse, partner, brother, sister or friend. It is the person who spurs you on, when that is required. I recall an entrepreneur telling the story of how he started his now highly successful business and brand.

> I was in my early twenties and working really hard travelling across the USA selling t-shirts and building the business. My girlfriend at the time was telling me to get a proper job and give up all the hours going into the business. The thing is, the business needed my energy and she needed my energy – one of them had to go!

Find the person who will spur you on; your supporter and motivator. This resource, almost always, comes for free.

Peers

Meet your peers – fellow start-ups – online on small business forums and websites and, offline, at events. The benefit is to share knowledge and, potentially, skills.

The benefit is to share knowledge and, potentially, skills

Small business forums

Visit websites, such as Enterprise Nation, to access free content, including practical tips and tools on all things start-up, as well as interviews with businesses a little ahead of you on the entrepreneurial journey. Meet fellow business owners on these sites and via the social media channels covered in Chapter 7. These are the most popular small business sites in the UK:

- Enterprise Nation: www.enterprisenation.com
- BusinessZone: www.businesszone.co.uk
- Startups: www.startups.co.uk
- Smarta: www.smarta.com
- StartUpDonut: www.startupdonut.co.uk.

There are also sites focused on particular sectors such as:

- Tamebay (for the e-commerce sector): www.tamebay.com
- Creative Boom (for creatives): www.creativeboom.co.uk
- The Design Trust (for designers): www.thedesigntrust.co.uk

Small business events

Head out to events and meet-ups to find like-minded people, fellow start-ups and potential partners for your venture. Find event listings on the sites outlined above and search Eventbrite and Meetup.com to track events happening in your area or sector:

- Eventbrite: www.eventbrite.co.uk (@eventbriteuk)
- Meetup: www.meetup.com (@meetup)

Join Enterprise Nation and attend free fortnightly member meet-ups to create your own support network.

Skills swap

Having found your network, consider swapping skills as a route to source the services you need – and to get your own skills known and talked about. This is an approach that has worked well for marketer, Paula Hutchings:

My first experience of skills-trading was in Sydney when I first set up Marketing Vision Consultancy. I wanted a website for my new business, but I was short of funds, so I didn't really want to pay for it! I was lucky enough to find a web designer who was willing to build the site for me in return for marketing support with a side business of his. This trade worked out really well. I went on to trade for graphic design work, photography and even hair-cuts! It helped me to get things I needed for the business when funds were tight, but it also helped me to gain valuable experience when I was just starting out. I still skills-trade now, if the right opportunity arises. To me it is important to support small business and start-ups in the same way that people supported me when I first set up. It is also a great way to make new contacts.

With a working knowledge of how to get this right, Paula suggests that, for a successful trade of skills, you need:

- a mutual trust between both parties to deliver on their promises
- an upfront agreement of exactly what each party will be delivering for the other
- consideration of the monetary value of each party's services, to ensure an equal trade
- a commitment to meeting agreed deadlines.

Source: Shutterstock.com, © Mathias Richter

Beware, though, the tax treatment of skills-swapping. Emily Coltman is chief accountant at FreeAgent and says:

> *My view is this would be taxable. In the case of offering marketing services in exchange for a website, the marketer should include the value of the marketing services provided to the web designer as part of their sales, but they could also include the value of the website as part of their costs. So the net effect on the profit is £nil.*

> *Ditto for the web designer, the other way round – the website value would be part of his/her turnover, the marketing services value would be part of his/her costs.*

> *Why not just leave them both out, because the net effect on profit is £nil and no cash changes hands? Because the barter transaction would count as part of sales for VAT purposes! So, if it's left out, the turnover – either when assessing how much to charge VAT on, or, if the providing business isn't registered for VAT, when monitoring turnover to see if registration is due or imminent – would be too low. My advice, even though the net effect on profit is nil, is to record the transaction as part of your sales.*

Beware, though, the tax treatment of skills-swapping

Having seen the benefits first hand, Paula now shares her marketing skills and knowledge, for free, for Enterprise Nation members. No recording on sales required here, as it comes as part of your membership!

With a background in marketing for top global brands, Christina Richardson could see a change in how small businesses were going about their marketing activity – and she could see sharing and collaboration playing a key role.

Case Study

Name: Christina Richardson

Business: Brand Gathering

Getting people to know about your business can be tough – especially on a tight budget – but by working in a number of entrepreneurial businesses and starting a few myself, I found that savvy business owners were finding a different way to reach new customers and market their brands. They were working together on their marketing.

This was the light-bulb moment. I decided to create an online tool that matches businesses by the customers that they want to reach, and they can strike up partnerships to sell together, cross promote each other, run events together, even create whole campaigns and products together. That's when Brand Gathering was born and the collaborative marketing revolution began.

Brand Gathering has built a strong community in a short space of time. Small businesses visit the site, use the BrandMatch tool and find a complementary partner with

▶

---

whom to run an activity. No expensive advertising or marketing campaigns required.

From shared retail pop-ups, to co-created products and simple cross-promotions, hundreds of savvy brands are collaborating to boost their sales and marketing results in the Gathering every day.

Being part of the Gathering is free, with options to pay for monthly subscriptions to carry out specific searches or get help from a GatheringGuru.

www.brandgathering.com

@brandgathering

Staff

Make the most of the appetite from young people to start their own business and hire them into yours, so they get experience of working with a start-up from the ground up. Find entrepreneurial talent through contacting schools direct or profiling your new venture on the sites students are visiting.

Go back to school

Approach your local school or college and offer to speak at the business class, to meet the young talent interested in your start-up. Check out these links and resources to make direct contact:

- **Speakers for Schools (www.speakers4schools.org)** – created by Robert Peston, this has grown into a network of over 850 speakers who give time to deliver business talks in state schools across the UK.

- **School Speakers (www.schoolspeakers.co.uk)** – founded by entrepreneur and former *Apprentice* contender, Claire Young, this business connects schools and colleges with speakers for business and enterprise classes. Get your name on the list to address the future entrepreneurs of your area.

- **Founders4Schools (www.founders4schools.org.uk)** – a free service for teachers from secondary schools across the UK that connects the school with local business owners and start-ups who are willing to speak on the topic of entrepreneurship.

- **Tenner (www.tenner.org.uk)**– the brainchild of social entrepreneur Oli Barrett, and now managed by Young Enterprise, Tenner is a nationwide competition that provides students with £10, which they have to invest in a start-up and deliver a return, in the space of a month.

  The Tenner Challenge is for young people who want to get a taste of what it's like to be an entrepreneur. It gives them a chance to think of a new business idea and make it happen, using real money to take risks in the business field, make a profit – and make a difference.

- **Apps for Good (www.appsforgood.org)** – looking for an up and coming app developer? This is the programme for you! A course for students, aged 10 to 18, on how to identify problems and build an app to solve that problem. An annual award sees winning ideas go on to be commercially developed and sold.

- **Gazelle Colleges (www.gazellecolleges.com)** – a network of 23 colleges across the UK, committed to creating the conditions to enable their students to leave education equipped with specialist skills and business skills, too.

- **Aldridge Academies (www.aldridgefoundation.com/ academies)** – supported by a foundation created by entrepreneur, Sir Rod Aldridge, these six academies have a specific focus on entrepreneurship.

  Our definition of the entrepreneurial mindset is one 'which strives to take action, solve problems, and rejects the status quo'. The attributes that we reward in students and prioritise in all our work are passion, creativity, teamwork, risk taking, determination, discipline, problem solving and vision.

There is opportunity to get involved in these projects that are working to cultivate and support the next generation of entrepreneurs. Right now, these young wannabes could be interested in working with you and your start-up to get hands-on experience!

Recruit online

Visit **www.plotr.co.uk** to create a profile for your start-up that will be viewed by thousands of young people considering their future. Plotr is a new online careers platform for 18 to 24 year olds, offering guidance on the most suitable careers for visiting students and a library of videos and content on how they can learn more/apply/get experience. Create a profile to be considered as one of their options.

Post a job for free on Enternships (**https://enternships.com**), which also attracts graduates and students looking for entrepreneurial openings. 'Dragon', Piers Linney, has launched a digital platform, **www.workinsight.org**, to connect employers like you with 14 to 19 year olds looking for workplace 'insights'.

In heading to schools, colleges and student platforms, you benefit from the skills and enthusiasm of a young member of staff and your new recruit benefits from the work experience which, with the introduction of an Enterprise Passport, will count towards their own future employability.

Outsource to the experts

When it comes to taking on experts to work on specific projects, look to the marketplaces and platforms outlined in Chapter 6 to find the talent you need, on a project basis.

Here are some steps to getting this relationship right.

- **The brief** – speak to any freelancer or professional and they will say, 'The better the brief, the better the result.' On marketplaces such as Elance and oDesk, there are example briefs but, if you aren't using these sites, include in your brief the purpose of the project, characteristics of your audience, the budget available and deadline dates. The more clarity you can

> ## @TheLordYoung calls for Enterprise for All
>
> The Prime Minister's enterprise adviser, Lord Young, released a report in late 2014 entitled 'Enterprise for All', recommending changes to the education system so students leave having developed the entrepreneurial skills they need. One of the recommendations is for an Enterprise Passport so, when approaching a young person with an entrepreneurial offer, you can highlight the benefit of the experience you are able to offer appearing on their passport.

offer, the quicker the freelancer can get to work and deliver a good job. If you are looking to brief a web developer, download the free website brief available on Sleeptwitch's website (**www. sleeptwitch.co.uk** – scroll to the end of the page).

- **Take references** – if you have not previously worked with a particular supplier, look for customer testimonials or ask if the supplier would be happy for you to speak to some of their customers.

- **Manage with care** – as the project starts, consider using project management tools to keep the project on track. See the technology below section for links to free project management software.

- **Build a team** – if the supplier continues to deliver top-quality work, consider giving them more! And perhaps even hiring them as part of the team, as the business grows.

The better the brief, the better the result

Look at my team!

Since meeting him at one of our events, I can often be found talking about Michael Litman and his company Brandsonvine – but most particularly about his 'About' page (**https://brandsonvine.com/about**). Michael is in the business of making short-form video ads for brands. Any company looking to do business with Michael will click on the site, view the portfolio and, more likely than not, head to the 'About' section to find out more about the people behind this particular company.

They will be met with an impressive board of profiles. Dig a little deeper and Michael will tell you, 'They are all friends. At some point, they have helped out in the business and I have their permission to include them on the profile page.'

The first impression for any potential customer is impressive. They do not need to know this team is not full-time nor located on one site. But it is what I love about small businesses; the art of looking professional and credible, with a little help from your friends!

Mentors

When it comes to finding a mentor, in my view, there are two types to find.

The first is 'the sounding board' – a wise and seasoned person who happens to be a good listener. As a business owner, you have most of the answers to the questions in your head. What you sometimes need is the opportunity to speak, which draws out your own conclusions. A listening mentor is an ideal route to achieving this. You do the talking, they do the listening, and you chart your own path.

The second type of mentor is a practical expert to whom you turn when you have a specific question that needs a sufficiently specific answer.

In terms of where to find a mentor, there are three options:

1. **DIY** – it is all about getting out and about to as many events as you can, where potential mentors might be. Take business cards, enter into conversations, and you could be surprised by what you find.

2. **Inhouse** – visit the Enterprise Nation marketplace (**www.enterprisenation.com/marketplace**) to search for big companies making their own staff available as mentors and advisers. Be matched with a marketing mentor from Unilever or a Digital Eagle from Barclays; just two of the types of skills on offer from large companies that increasingly are opening up their own asset base of people, for the benefit of start-ups.

3. **Government assistance** – visit the MentorsMe website (**www.mentorsme.com**), created by government and now managed by the British Bankers Association as an online resource with links to organisations offering mentoring support.

Rated advice

The Enterprise Nation marketplace (**www.enterprisenation.com/marketplace**) is home to over 10,000 small business advisers and is the largest site of its kind. Search the advisers best qualified to help via geography, i.e. advisers located closest to you, or specialisms such as accounting, design, social media, sales and marketing. The marketplace is the only site on which to find advisers accredited to take part in the Government's Growth Vouchers programme (**www.gov.uk/apply-growth-vouchers**), which offers young businesses up to £2,000 in match funding to spend on advice. Advisers on the marketplace with the highest number of positive reviews appear first in the search results, so you could consider this the TripAdvisor for business advisers!

Entrepreneurs

If there is a leading entrepreneur in your sector whom you would just love to meet, then be cheeky and make contact. What have you got to lose? When contacting high-profile entrepreneurs, stress how their story has inspired you to start out on your own and ask for the chance of 20 minutes of their time, at a location of their choice, i.e. make it easy for them to say yes to meeting you. Returning to Philip Crilly, who was mentioned in Chapter 7 with hosting his gluten-free granola product launch at Greg Wallace's restaurant, Philip did not stop there. Never the shrinking violet, Philip reached out to others:

> I spent some time working with James Averdiek, the founder of Gü puddings, at his flat in Putney, and with Charlotte Knight from G'NOSH dips, so I guess a good tip is to reach out to people you admire – on Twitter or through contacts – and you will find they are usually happy to help.

Returning to another entrepreneur mentioned earlier in this chapter, Paula Hutchings has it all sorted when it comes to having her business network intact.

> I found it useful to have a couple of mentors to turn to when I felt the need, or just wanted to bounce some ideas off someone. A mentor doesn't have to be in your industry – just someone whose opinion you value. As well as this, I'm fortunate to have some strong business-minded friends who help with practical questions and an amazingly supportive husband. They've all helped to keep me on track.

As the business is in its early stages, opt for any free help you can find and swap skills. As budget builds, consider outsourcing and subcontracting work to other self-employed professionals as opposed to hiring staff outright. It is simply the best way to grow.

Opt for any free help you can find and swap skills

People management

With more people in your network, stay on top of relationships with interns, suppliers and mentors and stay on top of client work. Here are some free online options to help.

- **Basecamp** – a tool we use at Enterprise Nation and could not do without! Manage projects, deadlines, people and company progress. Try it free for 60 days.

- **Evernote** – a project management tool to organise your work and life. With Evernote you can keep articles from the press, notes and presentations in one place.

- **Dropbox** – share documents with the team and keep your own work in the cloud; this is an essential piece of kit for any start-up, working from a range of locations.

- **WeTransfer** – send big documents to team members, contractors, partners, for free.

- **iDonethis** – an evening email shows the team what you and they have done during the day. It also sends prompts, if jobs are not getting done!

- **Powwownow** – free conference calling for up to 50 participants where you just have to pay the cost of an 0844 call, which is added to your regular phone bill.

- **GoToMeeting** – a product from Citrix and part of a suite of products that also includes GoToWebinar and GoToTraining, enabling you to host meetings, webinars and training (free or paid-for) with people across multiple borders. We use GoToWebinar at Enterprise Nation to broadcast fortnightly webinars with experts and entrepreneurs and love this technology!

- **OmniJoin** – a product from Brother offers the ability to share notes, documents and whiteboards, host online meetings and record/replay, too.

Product	Price
Basecamp **https://basecamp.com**	Free trial for 60 days.

Evernote www.evernote.com	Free, with an option to upgrade to packages costing £4 or £8 per month.
Dropbox www.dropbox.com	The Basic package is free or upgrade to a Pro account for £7.99 per month.
WeTransfer www.wetransfer.com	Free or upgrade to WeTransfer Plus for extra capacity and protection for $10 per month.
iDonethis www.idonethis.com	Free for one person or upgrade to the business package for multiple team members at a cost of $5 per month.
Powwownow www.powwownow.co.uk	Free to use. You pay the cost of the call.
GoToMeeting www.gotomeeting.co.uk	Free 30-day trial and then £29 per month for the Basic package.
OmniJoin http://webconferencing. brother.co.uk/	Free 30-day trial and then £15 per month for the Lite version.

Total cost of hiring people:

Skills swap	£0.00
Mentors	£0.00
Team and project management software	£0.00
Meet with an inspiring entrepreneur	£0.00
Total:	£0.00

Total costs incurred to date:

Coming up with an idea	£0.00
Carrying out market research	£0.00
Writing a business plan	£0.00
Taking care of company admin	£20.00
Technology set-up	£2.50
Making sales	£4.50
Branding on a budget	£13.29
Finding space	£20.00
Hiring people	£0.00
Total:	£60.29

Chapter

10

Raising funds

When you bought this book, you will have realised from the cover that the main thrust is to show how you can start a business on a budget. I know it is possible, as I have done it and seen thousands more do the same.

When I was approached to write this book, I wanted to do so as I am a big believer in:

- starting a business while 'working 5 to 9', i.e. holding onto the day job/studies/childcare and building the business at nights and weekends
- starting a business on a budget – by accessing as much as you can for free and embracing technology
- making sales as fast as you can – to build cashflow and confidence
- growing the business through income as opposed to borrowings.

The reason I believe in these principles is because, if you follow them, you do not have to hand over equity in the business or get into a debt situation too soon. It is the most low-risk route to starting and growing a business and has never been so plausible as it is today.

You do not have to hand over equity in the business or get into debt too soon

But what I do accept is there may come a time in the company's development when you need to find the funds to take the business onto its next stage of development. If that time comes, here are the places to look. Again, we return to the three main pillars of start-up support in Britain:

- government
- big business
- peers.

Government

In 2012, the Government introduced the StartUp Loans programme. Two years on and over 20,000 start-ups have been supported to the tune of over £100 million. You can make an application to be considered for a personal loan and be matched with a mentor.

> *Our StartUp Loan programme is designed to give you the opportunity to discover whether you have a business in you; to help you to create a business plan; and then give you a loan to get started. You will get continuing support from your mentor, and your future will be in your own hands. The limits of your business will be up to you.*

> Lord Young of Graffham, Founder, StartUp Loans

There is a holding StartUp Loans Company, with money distributed via StartUp Loan distribution partners. My personal favourite is Virgin StartUp, as they take time to consider loan applications, match you with entrepreneurs experienced in your field, and facilitate introductions to other parts of the Virgin empire into which you can sell.

One loan beneficiary, Yucoco Chocolate, is now selling its chocolate product on Virgin Trains and another, Lexie Sport, in a collaboration with Virgin Active. This is the kind of value-add from a loan that you are after.

Big business

Look to big businesses to lend or invest as growth plans are realised. This comes in a number of guises: banks, accelerators and leasing.

Banks

The banks are worth approaching with a business plan and request. As is the trade body, the Business Banking Association, which has created Better Business Finance (**www.betterbusinessfinance.co.uk/finance**) as an online database of finance providers, including angels, regional funds and government schemes. Simply search by your geographic location, industry and the amount of finance required.

Accelerators

As outlined in the 'Space to collaborate' section in Chapter 8, these are spaces and support provided by large companies to incubate and accelerate start-ups. With many of them, finance comes as part of the package.

Leasing

Increasingly on offer from large businesses is the option of leasing products as opposed to buying outright and therefore a favourable financial deal for you.

In July 2014, Toshiba announced a new finance initiative to help small businesses better cope with IT spending. On announcement, the company said:

> By taking part in finance offerings, small businesses can now have access to the latest technology solutions available, but in a more affordable way. Products are usually available for a 24- or 36-month lease period, giving customers increased control over their IT spend.

Look out for leasing deals to manage cashflow while continuing to invest in capital.

Peers

Crowdfunding is on the rise and fast becoming one of the most popular forms of funding for small businesses as, not only do you raise the funds that you are after, but you also raise your profile in the process. There are three main types of crowdfunding:

1. **Reward** – this is where people fund your business in exchange for rewards.
2. **Equity** – this is where the crowd invests in your business in exchange for equity, i.e. a percentage of the business.
3. **Loan** – this is where you raise a loan and repay with interest.

Turn to crowdfunding websites, such as these, to get started with a project:

Source: Shutterstock.com, © Lightspring

- Crowdfunder: www.crowdfunder.co.uk
- Kickstarter: www.kickstarter.com
- Crowdcube: www.crowdcube.com
- Indiegogo: www.indiegogo.com
- Seedrs: www.seedrs.com.

Angels

Raising investment from angel investors means accessing capital as well as, hopefully, useful industry contacts who will influence the growth of the business. There are plenty of funds and investors eager to part with their money and back good ideas and, what is more, the Government has made it financially attractive for angels to invest through something called the Enterprise Investment Scheme (EIS). This scheme offers up to 30 per cent tax relief to investors, and the Seed Enterprise Investment Scheme (SEIS) offers individual income tax relief of 50 per cent and exemption from capital gains tax (CGT) on any proceeds of sale of a SEIS investment. To be a qualifying company for either EIS or SEIS, visit the HMRC website to ensure you meet the criteria and complete an application. The approval process can take up to three weeks, so it is advisable to do this before approaching investors.

EIS: **www.hmrc.gov.uk/eis**

SEIS: **www.hmrc.gov.uk/seedeis**

Before considering funding, take all the steps outlined to get your start-up launched, well-known and making sales on a bootstrap of a budget. It will stand you in good stead.

Total cost of raising funds:

Total: £0.00

Total costs incurred to date:

Coming up with an idea	£0.00
Carrying out market research	£0.00
Writing a business plan	£0.00
Taking care of company admin	£20.00
Technology set-up	£2.50
Making sales	£4.50
Branding on a budget	£13.29
Finding space	£20.00
Hiring people	£0.00
Raising funds	£0.00
Total:	£60.29

Chapter

Managing the money

After following the steps outlined in these pages, you should be in the happy position of sales coming in and reasonable costs going out. To stay on top of the books and manage your money, consider an accountant alongside accounting software packages. Most accounting packages are cloud-based, which means you can access records from anywhere and be safe in the knowledge that your financial data is being backed up and protected.

Here are the major providers and their price points.

Product	Cost/offer	Links
Intuit QuickBooks	30-day free trial followed by three product offerings of £9/£19/£20 per month	**www.intuit.co.uk/ quickbooks/ accounting- software.jsp** @intuituk
SageOne Accounts	30-day free trial and £10 per month thereafter	**http://uk.sageone. com/accounts** @sageuk
Sage One Payroll	30-day free trial and £5 per month thereafter for up to five employees	
FreeAgent	30-day free trial followed by £15 per month (sole trader), £20 per month (partnership), £25 per month (limited company)	**www.freeagent. com** @freeagent

KashFlow	14-day free trial followed by £18 per month	**www.kashflow. com** @kashflow
Xero	The company states 'free trial and pay nothing until you are ready' – when you are, it is £19 per month	**www.xero.com** @xero

These tools, alongside accountants, will help with calculating cashflow and keep you safe in the all-important knowledge that there is more money coming in from sales, than going out of the business in the form of costs.

My advice would be to review the figures every week. What you want to know is:

- how much is in the bank
- what is owed to you in outstanding balances
- what you owe to suppliers/staff/partners
- what sales and outgoings are coming up within the next three months (this will be flexible, as new contracts and opportunities come online).

Review the figures every week

Over time, you may outsource this to an accountant or financial member of the team but, as the business owner, it is always your responsibility to know the finances of the company and, with cloud tools like those referenced above, it is easy to keep track.

As your start-up continues to grow, you will get busier and busier! Keep things in perspective and try to dedicate your time across three core aspects of the business. They are:

1. **Business development** – attracting new customers and trade by increasing sales channels/partners/routes to market and raising your profile so many more customers get to hear about you and visit to buy.

2. **Customer service** – taking care of existing customers through delivering a quality service or product on time and in budget. Keep in touch with customers through a regular newsletter, reward loyalty with deals and offers, and keep innovating to bring fresh ideas and products to market that get you noticed.

3. **Admin** – this is all about invoicing on time and settling invoices on time; in short, keeping on top of the books of the business.

You certainly will not enjoy all three tasks to the same extent. Maybe you love going out to make sales but do not enjoy so much the back-end admin of invoicing for those sales. That is okay. What is important is to imagine these three tasks as spinning plates – your job is to pay equal attention to keep them spinning!

Starting and growing a business is one of the most pleasurable experiences in life. You are master or mistress of your own destiny, running your own show and earning your own keep. You get to make money out of doing what you love and, as this book shows, it has never been so cheap to do just that.

Starting and growing a business is one of the most pleasurable experiences in life

Everyone loves a start-up, so get out there, be cheeky, beg, borrow, barter, get started and relish every moment of your entrepreneurial journey!

What did you think of this book?

We're really keen to hear from you about this book, so that we can make our publishing even better.

Please log on to the following website and leave us your feedback.

It will only take a few minutes and your thoughts are invaluable to us.

www.pearsoned.co.uk/bookfeedback

Appendix 1
Summary of start-up costs

Item	Cost
Idea	
Idea generation	£0.00
Friends and Family Focus Group	£0.00
Coming up with a name	£0.00
Market research	
Online search	£0.00
Industry trade reports	£0.00
Research at Business & IP Centre libraries	£0.00
Online surveys	£0.00
High-street surveys	£0.00
Business plan	
Produce business plan	£0.00

▶

Admin	
Company set-up:	
Consult with accountant	£0.00
Register as sole trader	£0.00
Register as limited company	£15 (via online at Companies House)
Notify landlord/local authority, etc.	£0.00
Insurance	£5.00 (for one month)
Intellectual property	£0.00 (to ascertain copyright)
Technology set-up	
Broadband	£2.50 per month
Wi-Fi	£0.00 (free hotspots)
VoIP phone	£0.00
Office software	£0.00 (based on free trial)

Sales	
Online:	
Via blog	£0.00
Via marketplaces	£0.00 (pay commission on sales or listing fee of 15p (Folksy), $0.20 (Etsy) or new partner fee (NOTHS))
Via template website	£0.00
Domain registration	£4.50
Offline:	
Shop share or pop-up based on commission	£0.00
Free space at trade shows	£0.00
Partnerships with complementary brands	£0.00
Meet face to face with customer	£5.00 (cost of coffee)
Branding	
Logo	£3.30 (or $5.00)
Business cards	£9.99
Social media	£0.00
SEO	£0.00
Email marketing	£0.00
PR	£0.00
Events, competitions, awards	£0.00

▶

Space	
Home office	£20.00 (fixtures and furnishings)
Out of home work/trading space	£0.00
People	
Skills swap	£0.00
Mentors	£0.00
Team and project management software	£0.00
Meet with inspiring entrepreneurs	£0.00
This book	£12.99
Bottle of bubbly to celebrate	£10.00
Total start-up costs	£88.28

These costs are based on month one set-up and start-up costs and don't take into account the cost of securing stock or supplies. It does show how you can be up and running in business for less than £100.

Appendix 2
Free tools

Market research	
Google	**www.google.com**
Bing	**www.bing.com**
Trade bodies	Various, and depends on your sector
Alibaba.com	**www.alibaba.com**
Business & IP Centre at British Library	**www.bl.uk/bipc**
DueDil	**www.duedil.com**
IMRG	**www.imrg.org**
Keynote	**www.keynote.co.uk**
Marketest	**www.marketest.co.uk**
Mintel	**www.mintel.com**
Office for National Statistics	**www.ons.gov.uk**
Trendwatching	**www.trendwatching.com**
YouGov	**www.yougov.co.uk**
SurveyMonkey	**www.surveymonkey.com**
Wufoo	**www.wufoo.com**
Find free Wi-Fi	
The Cloud	**www.thecloud.net/free-wifi**

O2	www.o2.co.uk/connectivity/free-wifi
BT	www.btwifi.com/find/uk
VoIP	
Skype	www.skype.com
Vonage	www.vonage.co.uk
Cloudapps	
Office 365	www.microsoft.com/office365
Google Docs	docs.google.com
Gmail	mail.google.com
Dropbox	www.dropbox.com
Google Analytics	www.google.com/analytics
Hootsuite	www.hootsuite.com
Evernote	www.evernote.com
Trello	www.trello.com
Basecamp	www.basecamp.com
MailChimp	www.mailchimp.com
Blogging	
Blogger	www.blogger.com
WordPress	www.wordpress.com
Tumblr	www.tumblr.com
Tweetreach	www.tweetreach.com
Payment tools	
PayPal	www.paypal.co.uk
Stripe	www.stripe.com
Worldpay	www.worldpay.co.uk
Sagepay	www.sagepay.co.uk
WP eCommerce	Wordpress.org/plugins/wp-e-commerce
Gumroad	www.gumroad.com

Marketplaces	
eBay	**www.ebay.co.uk**
Elance	**www.elance.com**
Enterprise Nation Marketplace	**www.enterprisenation.com/ marketplace**
Etsy	**www.etsy.com**
Eventbrite	**www.eventbrite.co.uk**
Folksy	**www.folksy.com**
iTunes	**www.itunes.com**
iStock	**www.istock.com**
Notonthehighstreet.com	**www.notonthehighstreet.com**
Amazon	**www.amazon.co.uk**
PeoplePerHour	**www.peopleperhour.com**
Yumbles	**www.yumbles.com**
Website builder	
Moonfruit	**www.moonfruit.com**
Wix	**www.wix.com**
Weebly	**www.weebly.com**
Shopify	**www.shopify.com**
Squarespace	**www.squarespace.com**
Social media	
Twitter	**www.twitter.com**
Facebook	**www.facebook.com**
Pinterest	**www.pinterest.com**
Instagram	**www.instagram.com**
LinkedIn	**www.linkedin.com**
YouTube	**www.youtube.com**
Vine	**www.vine.com**

Website metrics	
Google Analytics	**www.google.com/analytics**
Clicky	**www.clicky.com**
Crazy Egg	**www.crazyegg.com**
Social Blade	**www.socialblade.com**
Email marketing	
MailChimp	**www.mailchimp.com**
Constant Contact	**www.constantcontact.com**
Sign-Up.to	**www.signupto.com**

Appendix 3
Free small business support

Enterprise Nation	**www.enterprisenation.com**
BusinessZone.co.uk	**www.businesszone.co.uk**
Startups	**www.startups.co.uk**
Smarta	**www.smarta.com**
StartUpDonut	**www.startupdonut.co.uk**
Business is GREAT	**www.greatbusiness.gov.uk**
Tamebay	**www.tamebay.com**
Creative Boom	**www.creativeboom.co.uk**
The Design Trust	**www.thedesigntrust.co.uk**
Microsoft Small Business	**www.microsoft.com/en-gb/ business**
BT Small Business	**www.insight.bt.com/en/ hot-topics/start_up**
HSBC Knowledge Centre	**www.knowledge.hsbc.co.uk**
London*loves*Business.com	**www.londonlovesbusiness. com**
Elite Business	**elitebusinessmagazine.co.uk**
Telegraph Business Club	**www.telegraph.co.uk/ finance/businessclub**
Shell LiveWIRE	**www.shell-livewire.org**
Open to Export	**www.opentoexport.com**

Guardian Small Business Network	**www.theguardian.com/ small-business-network**
Real Business	**realbusiness.co.uk**

Index